C000146957

THE Extra IN THE Ordinary

THE Extra IN THE Ordinary

Thoughts on *friendship*, *family* and *faith*

David McLaughlan

Copyright © David McLaughlan 2013

Published 2013 by CWR, Waverley Abbey House,
Waverley Lane, Farnham, Surrey GU9 8EP, UK.
CWR is a Registered Charity – Number 294387 and a
Limited Company registered in England – Registration
Number 1990308.
The right of David McLaughlan to be identified as
the author of this work has been asserted by him in
accordance with the Copyright, Designs and Patents
Act 1988.

All rights reserved. No part of this publication may be
reproduced, stored in a retrieval system, or transmitted,
in any form or by any means, electronic, mechanical,
photocopying, recording or otherwise, without the prior
permission in writing of CWR.

For list of National Distributors see back of book.

Unless otherwise indicated, all Scripture references are
from the Holy Bible: New International Version (NIV),
copyright © 1973, 1978, 1984, 2011 by the International
Bible Society.

Concept development, editing, design and production
by CWR
Cover image: Fotosearch
Printed in China by 1010 Printing International
ISBN: 978-1-85345-959-7

1 *The Minister's Chair*

Harry's church has a new minister and he's young. Once installed, he wasted no time in ripping out the old pews and (to the shock of some parishioners) even the pulpit.

Don't get me wrong, I'm not against the church modernising – and Harry tells me that attendance has risen and the congregation is much more involved in the community than it used to be. But he still couldn't resist a souvenir from the old days, and I smiled when I saw it. In exchange for a donation to the church's mission fund, Harry had 'bought' the old, straight-backed chair that had stood in the vestry since he was a boy.

Much as I was sure the church would put his donation to good use, I did have to question his wisdom. The chair, fine-looking as it had undoubtedly once been with its intricately carved back and leather-covered arms, was scuffed and scored. One of the spindles in the back was cracked. It wouldn't match the furniture in Harry's house, and I dared to suggest that it didn't look all that comfortable.

'You're probably right,' he conceded as he walked round it. He looked quite emotional for a moment, and then he said: 'But think of all the thoughts of God that have been thought in it!'

It was my turn to concede. There are many different ways to be comfortable, and resting in thoughts of God surely has to be one of the best!

Yes, my soul, find rest in God; my hope comes from him.
PSALM 62:5

2 *A Battle Worth Losing*

If I fall out with my wife for more than a day or two, I usually end up exhausted.

Why? Because I'm awake half the night keeping an eye on myself. I have to make sure I'm turned away from her. I have to make sure I'm on the very edge of the bed, as far away from her as possible. I have to make sure I don't reach out to her in my sleep.

It's not easy because, you see, I was made for her. I was made to hold her in my arms. I was made to treat her better than sometimes I want to. Fighting against that leaves me miserable and shattered. But I'm stubborn!

We are made for heaven but so often I fight against that, too. I am determined to live life my way! Well, one day it might gain me wealth and earthly prestige, but my soul gets weary in the struggle.

I need to stop fighting battles I really don't want to win. A man hates to lose, but ... to be beaten by love is not so bad – and it does refresh the soul!

Let's put our stubbornness aside and be what we were made to be. Love your enemies and I'll love my wife. We will all be so much closer to heaven – and I'll get a good night's sleep!

All this is from God, who reconciled us to himself through Christ and gave us the ministry of reconciliation.
2 CORINTHIANS 5:18

3 *Under The Lintel*

My home town used to consist of an abbey and the farms and mills that supported it. Then along came the Reformation and the abbey was torn down.

Actually, it was burned out and left to fall down. Actually … it wasn't exactly left to fall down. As the town started growing around the blackened remains, the townsfolk found them a plentiful source of building materials.

So, anyway, the abbey came down, stone by stone, and the town rose up, incorporating those very same stones. Not surprisingly, some architectural oddities can still be found in unexpected places. The ruins that survived made a happy playground for children of my generation but are now preserved for their historical interest.

My grandparents grew up in a tenement row that stood in front of what would once have been the abbey's main entrance. Often, families of nine or ten would inhabit a single room. Several of these dwellings shared one particular stairwell and the doorway to it – and it's that doorway I want to tell you about.

Generations of men set out through it in the mornings and the evenings, heading for the mines or the ironworks or the mills. Local legend says it was a tradition to slap the lintel stone over that doorway each time they made it safely home.

Generations of women brought their meagre shopping home through that doorway and took their laundry to the 'steamie' through it.

Barefoot children would have been in and out of that doorway all day every day.

I like to think of a young lad and a young lass kissing in that doorway, under that lintel, before marrying and raising the family that produced the grandchildren and great-grandchildren who adored them and were so glad they met.

Why am I talking about doorways? What does a lintel stone have to do with anything?

Well, that stone, like every other stone in the poor, run-down (and, thankfully, now demolished) building came from the ruins of the abbey. And it must have had a prominent position there at one time.

Some unknown mason had carved five words of Latin into it. Words that obviously meant a lot to the monks who used to live in the abbey. Words that were no less applicable to the families now living hard, ordinary but no less wonderful lives where the abbey once stood. Words that you and I can take to heart in our everyday walk, even today.

They became the motto of my home town and they are: *Sine Te Domine Cuncta Nil.* 'Without You, Lord, it would all be for nothing.'

For the men coming home after a dangerous day's work, those words perhaps provided the strength to go out again the next day. For the constantly weary women, they might have been what kept a smile on their faces and courage in their hearts.

For me, that stone is a reminder that, while God does good work through great abbeys, His best work is done in humble homes.

Jesus replied, 'Anyone who loves me, will obey my teaching. My Father will love them, and we will come to them and make our home with them.'
JOHN 14:23

4 *Paved – With Gold*

Which road is it that's paved with good intentions?
Yeah, that's the one.
Julie, my wife, and I were in a bookshop/
coffee house. I'd been browsing the shelves while she
found us a table.

Turning round, I saw an elderly woman trying to reach a
vacant seat. She walked slowly and determinedly, leaning
heavily on two sticks and wobbling between steps.

She looked as if she would rather get there under her
own steam than be helped, so I stood and watched.

And as I watched I noticed a couple halt their coffee
cups inches from their lips. Without looking down, the
man shoved the bag at his feet further under the table –
out of the way, I guessed, in case he had to move quickly.

I noticed the waitress go over to wipe down a table
near the one the woman was heading for. An already
spotless table.

I noticed a young man, returning from the counter,
walk aimlessly for a few seconds, getting no closer to his
own table but getting no further away from the woman
should she need his help.

As it happened, nothing happened. She made it to her
seat without incident. And everyone relaxed.

Good intentions get a bad reputation sometimes – they
line more roads than just that notorious downwards one.
And, as I saw in that coffee shop, when the road we walk
is a hard one, God makes sure we are surrounded by way
more good intentions than we are ever aware of, or could
even imagine!

Remind the people to be subject to rulers and authorities, to be obedient, to be ready to do whatever is good.

Titus 3:1

5 Heirlooms

'When God sees how we treat His world, He must sometimes wish He hadn't made us!'

We'd been talking about environmental damage and my companion was indignant. I briefly wondered if she was right, and then my mind drifted to a family gathering a few years back.

Two generations of adults were chatting in the living room, while children, aged from four to 14, lounged about, teased each other, explored or ...

There was a crash from the kitchen!

Everyone fell silent. My sweetheart's hand went to her mouth – she had realised that the only child unaccounted for was ours: six-year-old Josh. Worse than that, she knew exactly what there was in the kitchen whose violent demise would make that noise.

We all rushed in and found a shocked Josh standing amidst the shattered remains of his granny's crystal fruit bowl.

Without hesitation, his granny swept him up into her arms and made sure he was OK.

'Oh, Mum!' cried Julie. 'How can you be so calm?

That bowl was your family heirloom!'

Her mother just shrugged. 'And so is Josh.'

I'm sure she would have rather our boy hadn't smashed her precious bowl, but she didn't love him any the less because he had. Likewise, I am sure there are a lot of things God would rather we didn't do to His world. And we should take note of that, for our own sakes as much as anything.

But I can't help thinking we are always going to be His family heirlooms!

In the same way your Father in heaven is not willing that any of these little ones should perish.
MATTHEW 18:14

6 *Whose Hands Are These?*

G rant sings with the praise band at our church. I don't know which I enjoy more, the sound of his singing or the smile he wears as he does it.

He gets around in a motorised wheelchair. His one good arm manipulates the joystick well but it isn't so great at holding things. So, when he finishes singing he goes over to Alex, and Alex raises a cup of juice and he drinks it.

Alex's wife also uses a wheelchair, and while both she and Grant are capable, smart people, they both occasionally need the service of legs or arms with finer motor control. So, Alex's able body does what he needs it to do – and also what two other people sometimes need it to do! It's a special kind of love to give others the day-to-day use of your limbs.

Watching him hold that cup for Grant reminded me of a story from wartime France. A bomb fell into a church. It didn't explode, but it brought several rafters down and one of them crashed in front of a statue of Jesus, breaking off its hands and its feet.

After a lot of consultation, the parishioners decided against having the statue repaired. It didn't seem necessary – after all, they were the Lord's hands and feet in this world themselves.

Alex, in his own way, was actively living that philosophy.

And if any of us are only using our hands and feet for ourselves, they are being woefully under used!

For who is greater, the one who is at the table or the one who serves? Is it not the one who is at the table? But I am among you as one who serves.
Luke 22:27

. . . .

7 *The Manufacturer's Way*

Derek had been seconded to the health and safety department of a local council. It was based in an old mansion house, where there was a huge chandelier in the front hall.

Once a year, the hall would be cordoned off, scaffolding would be erected and members of the staff would climb up to dust and check this beautiful ornament.

First, though, they had to go on a scaffolding safety course. They all had to wear hard hats and safety harnesses, of course, and an H&S expert would supervise them to make sure they didn't take any silly risks. It was a complex and expensive operation.

Then Derek found the box with the handle in it.

Naturally curious, he looked in the attic and spotted the mechanism the handle belonged to – the mechanism that lowered the chandelier to the floor!

Thereafter, this was how the chandelier was cleaned.

Some time later, recalling the occasion, he found one of the H&S guys surprisingly unimpressed.

'Our way worked fine,' he muttered.

'Yeah,' Derek agreed, 'but the manufacturer's way worked better.'

It's a truth that applies to more than just chandeliers. If you want to make a difference to the world, or even to your own life, you could try doing it your way; but the manufacturer's way will always be better. So, why not seek God's opinion first?

And Jesus? Well, He's the handle that keeps the whole world turning. So, don't put Him in a box and forget about Him. Once you find Him, hold on to Him!

Through him all things were made; without him nothing was made that has been made.
JOHN 1:3

8 Who's Guardian Who?

Peter had lived and worked in the town most of his life. Many of his family and friends were still there, but after he retired he had moved to a little village along the coast.

Still, it was summertime and his new home was very quiet. Meanwhile, there were too many barbecues going on in the old neighbourhood to ignore.

So, leaving the car at home, he took the train back up the coast and a friend met him at the station.

A good evening was had in the company of old mates, grilled food and more than a few beers. The storytelling and reminiscing went on, until finally Peter announced that he had to leave and get the last train home. There were offers of a lift to the station but he wouldn't hear of it. He didn't want to take anyone away from such a great party – and, besides, he knew the town and knew all the best short cuts.

But he'd forgotten that the quickest way was a dark path, away from any houses and not the kind of place where you'd want to get into trouble. Several people had been attacked there over the years.

As he walked, with the shrubs and trees blocking out the street lights, his party mood began to dissipate. He started to wonder if we really do have guardian angels. If we do, he hoped his was paying attention! If he met a 'bad guy' on this path, he would need all the help he could get ...

Then it happened. Out of the gloom up ahead, a figure emerged. Peter's heart started racing as all kinds of thoughts went through his head. Should he keep walking?

Turn and run? Jump into the bushes and phone for help?

This would be the perfect time for that guardian angel to appear, he decided. But it didn't.

The figure came closer – and stopped.

Peter gulped.

The figure said: 'Grandad?'

It was his fourteen-year-old grandson. He'd been out with friends and they had left him at the station with a four-mile walk to get home. He didn't have any money and his phone needed charging, so he couldn't ask his parents to pick him up. He had been really scared when he'd seen this figure approaching him on this dark path!

Laughing with relief (and remembering that statistically it was the teenage boy who was more likely to be assaulted), Peter turned his grandson round, walked with him to the station and paid for his taxi home. The boy's relief was so obvious, it had Peter smiling for the whole of his train journey.

He'd been hoping for a guardian angel to help him. The last thing he'd expected was for God to use him to help someone else. And someone he loved at that!

As far as his grandson was concerned, of course, I'm sure the difference between guardian angels and grandfathers was just a matter of a few feathers.

Then the angel of the Lord stood in a narrow path through the vineyards, with walls on both sides.
NUMBERS 22:24

9 Behind The Cobwebbed Window

The squat old building with the blistering paint had once been part of a whole row of buildings, but now it stood by itself. It seemed to have outlasted its neighbours through sheer obnoxiousness.

It had been a public house and, from its location and the stumps of the flagpole holders on its front wall, I guessed it had been a sectarian establishment – the kind of place you drank in only if your religion fitted.

At some time in its recent history, the upstairs rooms had been let out. I couldn't imagine they were any kind of comforting place to live.

Nowadays the door is boarded up and wire mesh covers the smashed ground-floor windows. The deep doorway is used as a late-night toilet, and the building fairly growls at passers-by, almost daring anyone to try to knock it down, let alone try to renovate it.

It has probably been decades since the upstairs windows have been cleaned, but that didn't stop me seeing someone looking out through the cobwebs. From across the street, on a rainy evening, I spotted him. I'm guessing it was a 'him' – teddy bears tend to be boys, don't they?

Where you have a teddy bear, I thought, you surely have a baby or a child. And you have the person who gave them the bear. Even in this most unpleasant of places, you have late-night cuddles and reassurance.

Amidst the drunkenness, the shouting, the aggression, the hatred, there had been love. Now there was desolation, the direct result, perhaps, of all that negative emotion and behaviour – but Teddy was still looking out. Waiting to love. Wanting to be loved.

It occurred to me that I know quite a few people like that.

They would deny it, of course, and probably punch me for suggesting it.

Often we run from our greatest need. When life makes it look like that need will never be fulfilled, it hurts so badly we deny we ever had it: we fight against it, bury it – and we become hard, obnoxious people in the process. We hurt others so we don't have to acknowledge our own hurt.

People like this, the human equivalent of that squat and dirty building, are the enemy Jesus told us to love. He told us to love them because it's the only thing that can save them. The pub is a masculine image, but it could just as easily be an embittered woman, or a damaged child.

And, all the while, their neglected souls will be looking out through their equivalent of that cobwebbed window.

It's not an easy thing to do, and we usually can't do it by ourselves, but ... Be careful, be prepared, be a surprise, always take God with you and open the door, go past the ugly facade, find that lonely teddy bear – and let love begin the renovation!

For the Son of Man came to seek and to save the lost.
LUKE 19:10

10 *Robertsianas*

I'd never visited Glasgow's botanical garden before, but we had a foreign guest living with us. Isn't it often the way that we need someone from elsewhere to show us what we have around us?

So, we strolled among the gardens, explored the maze and sweated in hothouses of various climates. Our visitor loved it.

Against all my expectations, I really enjoyed our time there. And, among all that exotic foliage, I couldn't help but notice one plant in particular: *Cyathea robertsiana*.

It wasn't the leaves that struck me, or the spectacular stalks, or the aroma. I'm really not a flower kind of guy! What attracted my attention was the descriptive plaque. Under a lot of Latin and technical terms, it told me that this tree fern grows best in disturbed ground – places where there had been a landslip, for example.

The Robertsiana grows quickly, its long, broad leaves shelter the ground beneath it and its widespread, interweaving roots are excellent at holding the soil together.

Just like people, some plants need a firm, secure grounding but others flourish in tricky circumstances, providing shelter and working quickly to stabilise things, making difficult situations less difficult.

I couldn't help but think of this as a metaphor for doing God's work.

I'm lucky enough to have a few friends who might easily be classed as Robertsianas. I hope you do, too. They truly grace God's garden!

Flowers appear on the earth; the season of singing has come, the cooing of doves is heard in our land.
Song of Songs 2:12

11 *May I Have This Dance?*

'Go and make me some disciples,' Jesus said. 'Yeah, I hear You, Lord, but ... Well, it's embarrassing talking about things like that to non-believers.'

Like a lot of people, I struggle with this issue. Then a child taught me a lesson.

Our church has quite a few little ones in it and they are very prone to dancing and clapping while the band and the congregation are praising God.

This particular Sunday, two brothers, their sister, Poppy, and a teddy bear made up the circle that was dancing around to *I Stand Amazed*. Little Poppy, who didn't look like she was quite four years old yet, kept looking into the congregation.

I followed her gaze and saw a bigger girl, sitting with her parents. Poppy mouthed this other girl's name each time the circle came round – but the girl didn't budge.

Looking a little concerned, Poppy passed the bear's paw to her brother and stepped out of the circle. She peered through the singing, swaying adults and gestured to her friend, 'Come on!'

Still no response. Surely she would give up?

But, no, she made her way through the forest of legs, stopped in front of her friend and tried to cajole her into joining the dance. Very nicely, the girl said no.

Poppy looked sooo sad!

Then, when she really should have taken the hint and walked away, she swallowed her disappointment, in a way that isn't easy for either kids or adults, held her hand out – and let it hang there.

Now, I have to explain that the bigger girl had a patch over one eye, because the other eye was lazy. Maybe that was why she didn't want to dance in front of everyone. Maybe that was why Poppy thought it important that she should.

And still her hand hung there.

The bigger girl leaned forward, squeezed her arm and whispered, 'I'll come up for the next song.'

Poppy went back and rejoined the circle for the last chorus of *I Stand Amazed* – which turned out to be the last song! The other girl never got to dance.

Now, both girls are children of faith-filled families and they will be fine, but I learned a lesson about making disciples.

I can stay in the dance, enjoying myself and ignoring those outside it. I can list all the things that prevent me from talking about my faith. And the people I might have been talking to may have just as many reasons for not listening if I had raised that awkward subject.

But at some point I need to step out of my comfort zone, stick my hand out and leave it hanging there. I can't make anyone *take* my hand, and normally that would be another good reason for not even offering it. But then Poppy reminded me that the music doesn't last forever.

Not everyone feels invited to join the dance. And if I don't ask them to, they may never have another opportunity.

Therefore go and make disciples of all nations, baptising them in the name of the Father and of the Son and of the Holy Spirit.
MATTHEW 28:19

12 *On A Cloud*

So, what do angels do all day? Sit on clouds playing harps? Fly around? Knit?

I prefer the last option. Not for all of them, of course. Just for the one who visited my friend Jackie.

Twenty years ago, she was a hairdresser expecting her first child. Her bump was an obvious topic of conversation with the customers.

Then a new customer came to the salon. While Jackie was doing her hair, the talk turned, inevitably and happily, to baby matters. Then the woman asked if her mum had been knitting lots of baby clothes.

Jackie said no. The woman asked if she had been knitting herself.

Jackie took a deep breath and explained. She loved hand-knitted baby clothes, but she couldn't knit. Her mum had died when she was only young, so there had been no one to teach her how to. Her mum would never see her baby, let alone knit clothes for him or her.

A week later, Jackie turned up for work to find a brown-paper package waiting for her. Inside was a pile of the most beautiful knitted baby clothes she had ever seen. There was also a note, which said: 'From your mum x'.

Jackie's bump is now a handsome young man – but she still has those clothes.

For the past twenty years, she's been looking out for that woman to say thank you, but she has never seen her again.

I imagine she's been busy. On a cloud somewhere. Knitting.

---

*The angel of the L*ORD* found Hagar near a spring in the desert; it was the spring that is beside the road to Shur.*
GENESIS 16:7

13 *Map And Compass*

In younger (fitter and sillier) days, I used to do a lot of hill walking. Occasionally, I would ignore all sensible advice and go off on my own. I enjoyed not leaving a route plan behind so that people could find me if I went missing. I enjoyed not knowing when I would be back.

That kind of freedom is fine – until something goes wrong!

I had come down from walking a ridge of hills expecting to find a bothy by a stream in the woods below. Bothies are old, abandoned cottages, often with dirt floors, and are considered luxurious if they have a door and a roof that keeps out the rain. They are sanctuaries in the wilderness.

I knew that this one was in good condition – but so did the youth group I found there! So, as I was trying to get away from crowds, I walked on.

That decision complicated the situation more than a little. There was another bothy, but it was quite a distance away. To get to it I would have to skirt a loch, go through some woods and then cross some difficult terrain. And, just to increase my panic levels, I guessed it would be dark an hour before I got there!

Now, there is no dark like middle-of-the-mountains dark.

Once I couldn't see the hills around me any more, I sat down on a tussock. I took a note of all the bearings I would need, measured the distances on the map and figured out how many paces I would need to walk on each leg of the journey.

Unable to see anything but my torchlit map and compass, and resolutely counting paces, I walked on. From point to point. With no idea if each point was actually the one I'd aimed for. It was the most hopeless way to travel.

When I'd finally walked as many paces as I reckoned, I stopped. I looked around. I couldn't see a thing. It was late, and I was right out of ideas.

On an impulse, I put my hand out – and touched the gable end of the bothy. It was so dark I could not see a building I had almost walked into.

Looking back now, I can't imagine why I reached out like that – unless the impulse came from above.

I was safe. I wouldn't be spending the night sleeping on

the grass with the sheep. But I would have been in big trouble if I hadn't had my map and compass.

In this benighted world, we need exactly the same things. And we have them. The map that shows us which way to travel is the Bible. The compass is that quiet voice in our hearts, the Holy Spirit. Oh, and of course I needed the torch so I could use them properly – and for a torch we have 'the light of the world', Jesus.

Together they will see us safely to the sanctuary at the end of our journey.

Since you are my rock and my fortress, for the sake of your name lead and guide me.
PSALM 31:3

14 *A Rubbish Reason For Believing*

The park had been full a few hours earlier. Half a dozen football matches were taking place at the same time, and each match had its supporters, trainers, managers and the rest. Almost everyone there was an adult. Just not adult enough to pick up after themselves ...

Now the park was empty – except for two guys in high-visibility jackets collecting and bagging the empty bottles and all the other rubbish left behind.

How must they feel, I wondered, about the people who

think nothing of dropping stuff at their feet and walking away without another glance?

Frustrated? Annoyed?

Probably not. Because if it wasn't for people like the litter droppers – well, there would be no need for litter picker-uppers, and those two guys might well be out of a job.

It's the same when we wonder why the world has so much pain in it, why there are so many folk who seem to think of kindness and decency as weaknesses.

If it wasn't for them – well, what need would there be for Christians?

One day, there will be a litter-free world. It will be arrogance-free, ignorance-free, hate-free, violence-free. But until then the God-loving folk will keep on picking up everyone else's rubbish and trying to sort it out.

It's in the job description. They're why we're here. We'll be unemployed one day, and we'll be happy about that. But until then let's be highly visible and let's get to work!

But I have raised you up for this very purpose, that I might show you my power and that my name might be proclaimed in all the earth.
EXODUS 9:16

15 *The Names Remained*

Sometimes when I'm writing I change names to spare people's blushes. I rarely change locations, but I'm sure my literary inspiration, H.L. Gee, (who died in 1977) did both.

Many times, I have Google-Mapped a location to which he refers only to find it doesn't exist. Of course, the changing of names doesn't change the truth of his stories.

Once, though, I was reading a book of his from 1955 in which he mentions a walking holiday he'd taken twenty years previously. He and a friend stayed the night – and a rainy day – at a farmhouse with a very distinctive name.

Let's call the gentleman he met there 'Old George'.

'And in the evening we talked in the kitchen,' Mr Gee writes. 'We also listened – listened to Old George as he chatted and joked by the peat fire, teaching us how to play [Nine Men's Morris], retelling old tales full of rich humour, and smiling at us in spite of the pain he suffered.

'A big man, Old George, who passed on at a ripe old age only recently. His face was a benediction, its ruggedness softened and illuminated by that gentle and lovely smile. He had a serenity which nothing less than the love of God could give.'

Because of the unusual name, I looked the farmhouse up. It was still a working farm and had recently gone back to taking in lodgers. It also seemed to be run by a family who shared the same surname as Old George!

So, I went to their website and sent them the most unusual 'booking request' they must ever have had, asking if they knew of the book and quoting to them from it.

I eventually got a short, uninterested response. The farmer's wife suggested that it might have been written by her husband's great-grandad, but she didn't know.

Well, I could have just left it like that – except I couldn't. I wrapped the book up and sent it to them.

No reply. Not for the best part of a year.

Then the farmer phoned me. He explained that his wife had framed the pages about Old George and hung them in the corridor outside the guest rooms. Each time he went up there to do some maintenance, he stopped and read them.

He confessed he'd always thought that faith was soppy stuff. So did most of his friends. So, while he often felt there was something more to life, he had never pursued it for fear of embarrassment.

But, from what he'd been told about his great-grandfather, Old George had been anything but soppy. He'd been a real man, in fact. And Old George's words talked to him each time he passed along that corridor.

So, why was he calling me? Because he had recently given his life to Jesus, and he wanted to thank me for sending the book to him. Of course, he understood when I said it wasn't me who sent it.

The thanks go to God – and to H.L. Gee, who, just for once, didn't change the names.

I am sending him to you for this very purpose, that you may know how we are, and that he may encourage you.
EPHESIANS 6:22

16 *Things We Found Inside Books*

There's a shop I know that sells second-hand books for charity. It's cosy and lined with shelves, it has a kids' area and it sells old LPs as well. But then so do lots of charity shops.

What makes this place stand out for me is its collection of 'things we found inside books'.

Stuck to its walls are bookmarks new and old, postcards, betting slips, an autograph from the Scottish comedian Rikki Fulton, a letter from a book club sent out 'on the occasion of the Coronation' and so on. Folded over to give a degree of anonymity were letters people had received and slipped into the books they'd been reading.

Of course, any child – or anyone who's ever been a child – will tell you there are other things to be found inside books, like adventure, mystery, instruction, fun, excitement.

If you can get all of those things from ordinary books, we should surely expect to get a bit more from the Bible. And we do. The Bible provides everything other books have to offer – plus an explanation for the whole universe. It tells us who we are, what we were made for and how we can accomplish it.

I'm sure people mark their place in the Bible with as unusual an assortment of bookmarks as ever might be found on the wall of that shop. They might even use a letter.

Of course, the Bible itself is a letter – a letter from God, telling us how much He loves us. Now, that really is something worth finding inside a book!

I write these things to you who believe in the name of the Son of God so that you may know that you have eternal life.
1 JOHN 5:13

17 *My Mirror*

Graham works in the menswear section of a big department store. It's an old-fashioned kind of place and the staff in his section do their best to treat their customers as gentlemen. But fewer and fewer men are used to that these days, so he's come to expect some unusual behaviour.

Like the man he had in the other day who needed a new suit for his niece's wedding. He admitted that he hated shopping for new clothes and it had been a long time since he had bought anything so formal.

Graham sized him up with a professional eye and picked out a few suits he thought would look good on him. The man tried them all on, but each time Graham steered him towards the full-length mirror, he resisted. At first, Graham thought he had such low self-esteem he couldn't bear to look at his own reflection.

But that wasn't it. Each time the man turned away from the mirror, he turned towards his wife.

Seeing her smile at Graham's puzzled look, the man explained: 'She's my mirror. After all, who else would I want to look good for?'

Telling me about it afterwards, Graham reckoned that it's a lucky, lucky man who finds a wife who suits him so perfectly. But, of course, as he reminded me, there is Someone who knows us even better than a 'significant other' ever could – and who else would any of us want to look good for?

May the presence of God be your constant mirror.

Look to the LORD and his strength; seek his face always.
1 CHRONICLES 16:11

18 *The Graveyard Sleeper*

I had been tempted to walk on by when I saw him leaning against the corner in a sad state of disrepair. It was a cold, wet night and I was in a hurry to get home. 'Of course,' a little voice said, 'it's just as cold and wet for him. Aren't you going to check he has a home to go to?'

So, I asked if I could help. The man pulled himself together and assured me he was just on his way to the hostel. Drink had cost him his job, his family and his home, but he was getting better and at least he wasn't sleeping in the graveyard any more.

I was at a loss as to how to respond. So, he went on. He told me the history of the graveyard, how in the days of Robert the Bruce and William Wallace several Scottish clans had gathered there before deciding *not* to march south.

Being a history buff myself, I knew this was all true; but he told me a lot more I didn't know. Then he asked me my surname. He declared it a good name – and told me the history of my clan. Again, he was spot on.

We had a fascinating chat. Then he shook my hand and shuffled off towards the hostel. And I was left thinking, once again, that God doesn't make ordinary people. Every one of His creations has a unique story – and we miss so much if we choose to walk on by!

When Jesus got out of the boat, a man with an impure spirit came from the tombs to meet him.
MARK 5:2

19 *A Tourist In The House Of God*

It was my first time in York Minster. It's a stunningly beautiful cathedral, but I felt a little awkward.

Here I was, a believer, walking around inside an awesome monument to God, but I wasn't there to worship. I had a bag dangling from one wrist and a camera swinging from the other.

Let's face it: I was a tourist in the house of my Lord.

York Minster is a working church, even though it's open to the general public. A service was finishing in front of the main altar as I arrived.

Just as I was starting to wonder if I was really showing enough respect, a member of the clergy began saying a prayer in one of the side chapels. I walked on by, but his words followed me.

He was wired for sound and there are speakers discreetly hidden all round the Minster. As I gazed at this and took a picture of that, his prayer – for people of faith, and those yet to come to faith, and the whole world – accompanied me. It would fade a little, then surprise me as I neared another speaker.

As I walked, those words of love warmed my soul and helped me to see things a little differently.

York Minster is impressive beyond words – but although men can put up some amazing piles of stone, their work doesn't even begin to compare with God's. Elaborate towers and spires reaching hundreds of feet into the air can't approach the wonder of even the weed at our feet. Delicately carved and gilded cherubs are nothing next to the poorest, dirtiest baby.

So, yeah, I was a tourist – I just had to accept that. But if I took anything from the experience (other than some stunning photos), it was the realisation that I should walk through the world the way I walked through York Minster. I'm only here for a short while (compared with eternity), so I'm going to do the tourist thing and go around wide-eyed with amazement.

But, more importantly, wherever I am in the world I need to learn to expect to hear the voice that warms my soul.

It won't be a minister speaking, it will be God. If I listen carefully, I should be able to hear Him around every pillar, and in every breath of wind, every whimper of fear, every laugh, every question from a stranger ...

Because He does love people of faith, and those yet to come to faith, and the whole world.

He even loves tourists!

Then the Lord spoke to you out of the fire. You heard the sound of words but saw no form; there was only a voice.
DEUTERONOMY 4:12

20 *Inviting God In*

I've been reading about Frank Laubach recently. He's not so well known in Britain, but in America he was the first and only missionary ever to have his face put on a postage stamp.

Through his 'Each One Teach One' programme, hundreds of thousands of children in the Philippines were taught to read and write, giving them a better chance in a difficult world.

However, the spiritual aspect of his mission seemed less productive. He was helping people in this world but not preparing them for the next. He was intensely lonely and felt a total failure.

Then, after years of struggling, he tried a different tack. Instead of reaching outwards, he turned inwards. He tried making space for God in each waking hour of the day; then every half-hour; then every fifteen minutes.

It wasn't easy. Often, he failed. But he persevered – with amazing results!

When God finally became his constant companion, he found himself evangelising less. He didn't need to – people were drawn to him. Previously, they hadn't wanted what they saw him trying to 'sell'; but now they wanted what he so obviously had himself!

God had put His stamp on the man whose image would later appear on ... a stamp!

How often do you let God into your day? Do you think you could invite Him in every hour, every half-hour and so on? It's an experiment that made a huge difference to Frank Laubach, and it might do the same for you!

Enoch walked faithfully with God.
GENESIS 5:24

21 *Almost Heaven*

I once heard a wise woman explain that being 'unselfish in God' was, paradoxically, the most selfish thing we could do. The benefits of a life of faith were actually quite embarrassing, she said. God was just so good to her!

It reminded me of a dream I'd had.

I had died and I was walking up the last stretch of the narrow, rocky path to heaven. I was out of puff, leaning on my knees each step of the way. It had been a long journey and I was exhausted – but I was so happy!

Then it all went wrong. I presented myself at the big gates, and Saint Peter welcomed me kindly and checked his list. He checked it again. My name wasn't there!

He apologised very sincerely, stepped back into heaven and closed the gates between us.

For a minute I stood there, considering how devastated I *ought* to be, and almost was.

Then I sat myself on a rock and looked back down the path I had been walking for the latter part of my life. And I realised that I was content. In fact, I would be content to sit there for all eternity, never getting into heaven but honoured beyond words to have been allowed to walk His path.

That's the kind of reward that comes from following Jesus. It is enough in itself.

But, of course, that was just a dream. The reality will be even more wonderful – and hopefully I'll actually get in!

But I said, 'I have laboured in vain; I have spent my strength for nothing at all. Yet what is due to me is in the LORD's hand, and my reward is with my God.'
ISAIAH 49:4

22 *The Pain Seat*

What's the kindest thing anyone has ever done for you? Luckily, I am spoiled for choice, but a little something that happened the other night is surely a contender.

The evening was so nippy I could see my breath on the air. I was popping in to see an elderly neighbour who hadn't been keeping so well. Pain in his lower back had kept him from being as active as he usually was, so I wanted to see if there were any errands I could run or anything else I could help with.

He looked in a bad way, though he insisted he was starting to feel better.

He invited me in and sat on the couch as he directed me towards the only armchair. It was draped in a woollen blanket, through which I soon felt the warmth of a hot-water bottle at the base of my spine!

I enjoyed it for a moment or two and then I realised: this chair was the old fellow's pain relief – and he had given it to me! I had to force myself to stay there, knowing he would be embarrassed if I insisted on swapping places.

I left him my phone number and promised I would pop in from time to time – but he had already given me more than I could give him.

Big acts of charity may make headlines but I think it's the little, unmentioned kindnesses like that one that really make the angels smile!

All these people gave their gifts out of their wealth; but she out of her poverty put in all she had to live on.
LUKE 21:4

23 *Still Shining Bright*

One of the best things about Saint Andrew's Church is the leaving of it.

I don't mean any disrespect, and I'm sure the rector and congregation would agree with me. You step outside the dear old building, cross a road and a strip of grass – and you're on the beach. Being Scotland, it's rarely warm, but the view of the sea and the islands off the coast is rarely less than spectacular!

Leaving church one Sunday, I walked towards the shore, lost in thoughts of the sermon and a little personal prayer. Then I looked along the sand and saw what turned out to be a sea baptism. A little community church was welcoming another lamb into its flock.

I wandered over and was quickly made welcome. Song sheets were handed out and we sang heartily against the wind as the brave initiate and her pastor waded out into the cold sea.

It was truly wonderful! Soon, she was welcomed back to dry land with a rousing round of applause, hugs, plenty of towels and a hot cup of coffee.

Afterwards, I chatted with a few of the people there. I confessed to one older man that the walk with God was a relatively new one for me.

'Ah, yes,' he said, waving a finger in my face. 'You still have that look about you.'

It was a profoundly discouraging moment! Walking away afterwards, I wondered what he had meant. Was this more experienced Christian telling me that the joy I felt in Christ would fade? That people could tell I was a believer by looking at me now, but the world would soon rub that shine off?

Dismay actually began to verge on despair.

Then I remembered the song we had all been singing as the sister I'd never met before had her sins washed away: *Amazing Grace!*

The man I'd been talking to had sung those words beside me. Hadn't he paid them any attention?

The hymn refers to how precious it is when we first believe, but then concludes:

'When we've been there ten thousand years, bright shining as the sun,we've no less days to sing God's praise, than when we first begun.'

This man could see I was fairly new to faith from something in my expression. That something was the love of God. Grace. Redemption. Will those things be any less wonderful in ten years' time? In twenty years? Ten thousand years?

I don't think so. So, it's down to me.

Should you meet me when I'm in my nineties, forty years from now, I hope I'll still be shining bright. I pray you will still see that joy in my face. And I may shed a tear of happiness if I see it in yours.

Because it really *is* that amazing. And, when it comes to eternity, we're all really just at the beginning of our walk with God.

Sing to the Lord, all the earth; proclaim his salvation day after day.
1 Chronicles 16:23

24 *Mend Or Pass By*

In 1653 – when I were but a lad – Izaak Walton, an ironmonger, wrote a book called *The Compleat Angler*. It was about – well, fishing. Walton was a keen fisherman and his intention was to provide a book of instruction for others similarly inclined. However, the incidental wisdom and faith contained between its covers have won it a much wider readership.

Back in those days, the arts of editing, proofreading, even spelling, weren't what they are now. Which is why, at the end of his introduction, the author begs the reader to 'shew himselfe courteous in mending or passing by some errors in the Printer, which are not so many but that they might be pardoned.'

Ah, if only we could extend such courtesy to each other!

We are none of us such perfect editions that we can fairly criticise anyone else. Some people's faults may be more blatant or more destructive than others, and in those instances we might step in and do some subtle editing where we can. Or if nothing can be done – and only then – we might pass on by with a prayer. Or, passing by, slow down and walk beside someone for a while.

Not one of us has so many errors that the One reading the book of our life will not forgive them, and we should aspire to do the same for others.

Especially bearing in mind that, for many of our books, there may well be a much better sequel.

But now, please forgive their sin – but if not, then blot me out of the book you have written.
Exodus 32:32

25 *Willingly Given*

When she was thirteen or so, my daughter Amy walked into Glasgow's Kelvingrove Art Gallery and Museum and exclaimed, 'Oh! This is my favourite museum!'

I was tickled that she actually had a favourite – and I have to admit that my favourite painting hangs in it.

Glasgow City Council bought Salvador Dali's *Christ of Saint John of the Cross* only a year or so after its completion. Since then, it has become one of the most famous, and the most valuable, paintings in the world. The council has turned down many offers of phenomenal amounts of money for it.

It depicts Jesus hanging on the cross, suspended in a thundery sky above a calmer, sunnier Sea of Galilee where his fishermen-disciples are at work. In a way, it's a reminder that God is always there, even when we are about our everyday business; but it is so much more than that.

One of the long-term problems the council has had with the painting is how best to display something so wonderful. More than once it has been vandalised, but they have kept it on display. Perhaps someone on the council has been aware of the spiritual good it does – or perhaps the public outcry would have been too great if they had hidden it away!

An information panel explains that Dali was inspired by a sketch done by a 16th-century monk known as Saint John of the Cross. It also explains something that most people never notice. The figure of Jesus is outstretched on the cross. He is definitely crucified.

His hands and feet are well lit. But there are no metal spikes, no nails!

After he had finished the painting, Dali said the idea for it had come to him in a dream, in which a voice had told him that nails and blood would spoil the image and so he must leave them out.

But is that the whole story? I think the voice may have had a further agenda.

For me, the lack of nails through Jesus' hands and feet has a very clear message. They are missing because they are not needed. Jesus' sacrifice was willingly offered. Nails may have been used – but Jesus hung Himself upon the cross. For us.

And that's my favourite part of my favourite painting in my daughter's favourite museum.

And being found in appearance as a man, he humbled himself by becoming obedient to death – even death on a cross!
PHILIPPIANS 2:8

26 *This Is My Mum*

G ary has been part of the MacCowan family for decades, ever since he was adopted at the age of eight.

I've known him for several years now, and I know his adoptive family well. But the other day, at church, he introduced me to someone I'd never met before.

'David,' he said, 'this is my mum.'

Luckily, I realised she must be his biological mother before I put my foot in it! We talked for a few minutes, then he eased her away to introduce her to others.

After the service, I saw her standing alone. She was wiping away a tear and I asked her if she was OK. She shook her head and admitted that she hadn't expected it to be like this. She explained that Gary had introduced her to everyone in the church, and every time he had said, 'This is my mum' she had heard nothing in his voice but pride. There was no recrimination for the fact that she had given him up, no anger that she had hardly been involved in his life. Despite all she was, and all she wasn't, Gary had still been delighted to have her there, and proud to introduce her as his mum.

She felt she didn't deserve it, and perhaps she didn't; but Gary wasn't going to let that stop him. He's a man of faith and I'm sure he knew that God would be glad his mother was there.

And I could just imagine God looking down with a smile and saying: 'This is my son.'

So in Christ we, though many, form one body, and each member belongs to all the others.

ROMANS 12:5

27 *Fallen But Standing*

If trees could think, this one must have wondered if it would survive the storm – or would the morning see it broken and useless, waiting to be cleared away, just so much firewood?

No doubt it clung to its position, straining to remain as it was. But some storms just will not be resisted, and when its roots started breaking, it must have felt – if trees *could* feel – like the whole world was tilting under it.

That was two years ago.

Now the tree lies at an angle of about forty-five degrees, its lower branches holding it off the ground, the underside of its roots exposed to the air.

Its sap still flows. Its leaves still grow. It still breathes in carbon dioxide and breathes out oxygen. Birds still sit in its branches and build their nests there. The tree serves all the purposes it used to. But now, perhaps, it has some new functions as well. Judging by the holes there, I'm pretty sure that several small creatures have burrowed out homes in the soft soil under its sheltering roots.

The tree is still a tree – but in a new position.

When storms hit our lives, we can't help but fear the worst – that all we are will soon come to an end.

I won't pretend it doesn't sometimes happen. But sometimes God just wants to move us to a different position; and sometimes, because we are bound by fear or habit, that requires a storm!

Then the Lord spoke to Job out of the storm.
Job 40:6

28 *Someone To Care*

John grew up at a time when the diagnosis for someone like him was 'not right in the head'. His family kept him away from medical interference – or help – because such things were shameful in those days.

By his sixties, he had outlived his family and could be seen around town looking ever scruffier and ever gaunter. He occupied himself supporting the local football team and being chief mourner at every funeral in town – whether he knew the deceased or not.

Then a man he didn't know started talking to him. The man invited him to lunch in a cafe, chatted like they were old friends and then, to John's amazement, arranged to meet him again the next week.

The lunches became a regular event. Sometimes, they would end with a visit to a clothes shop and John would go home with a new winter coat, or a pair of shoes.

I'm pretty sure John thinks he has a friend now. Someone to care about him again.

In a way, he does.

I grew up along the street from John and he used to terrorise us as children. He was older, stranger, and a bit dangerous. He tried to poke my brother's eye out with a lit match. He used to stalk my sister.

My dad had once confronted his, incensed by John's latest misbehaviour. The two tough working men stood nose to nose. My dad threatened to involve the police – and John's dad broke down in tears. He begged. John was all he had. He was all John had. He'd do his best. He'd keep John locked in the house. Whatever it took. 'Please, Davie. Don't take my son away from me!'

Dad relented, and told us to just stay away from him!

When I met John again in adulthood, he was struggling to find twenty pence to pay for something. I was tempted to take some pleasure in his difficulty, but I gave him the money instead. He didn't recognise me, but I let go of the hate I felt for him – and I felt better for it.

Later, I realised that God required much more from me for John than just that twenty pence.

Thinking back to that confrontation with my dad, I was touched by his old father's love. He'd looked after John for the rest of his days. An auntie took over after he died, but now she's gone, too. For most of his life, John has only ever had one person to look after him.

Now he has me.

Forgiveness is a big ask. But God asks more. 'Love one another' means no one being left uncared for in this world. And if He can't use friends, He'll use an old enemy.

John doesn't remember who I am, and I won't remind him. I don't know which of us will go first, but if things go my way I'll be the chief mourner at his funeral: for the old days, for his dad, and for the love of God, whose son John also is.

Make sure that nobody pays back wrong for wrong, but always strive to do what is good for each other and for everyone else.
1 THESSALONIANS 5:15

29 *The Heart Of The Compass*

When you take children to a maritime museum, they just have to climb to the bridge of every boat there and spin the big steering wheel! On one old puffer, though, it was the ship's compass that captured *my* attention.

It was an impressive piece of work. The circular brass plate was finely engraved with the thirty-two points of the compass and every degree in between. There was a starburst in the middle and an intricate, scalloped pattern around the circumference. The wooden case and glass dome were beautifully made, though years of hard use had left them chipped and scratched.

But most of that really was just decoration. The heart of the compass was the narrow strip of magnetised steel – pointed at both ends, painted red at one – which, despite all the turbulence the wind and the sea could inflict, obeyed the invisible force that kept turning it in the right direction.

Your life may be an impressive piece of work. It may be carefully crafted and artfully presented. But all of that is superficial stuff. What matters, in the storms and calms of life alike, is whether your heart spins aimlessly or turns in the right direction under the constant influence of that invisible force.

Nothing will stop kids wanting to swing the steering wheel. But each of them has their own compass that will automatically turn in God's direction, and we just have to encourage them to turn with it!

In everything set them an example by doing what is good. In your teaching show integrity, seriousness and soundness of speech.
TITUS 2:7–8

30 *Be The Band*

I had to hide my surprise when Clara told me she had been part of the working party giving her church a much-needed makeover. With the best will in the world, she isn't the sort of woman I can imagine up a ladder slapping on paint, so I delicately asked what particular job she had done.

'Oh, I played the organ,' she replied happily.

Seeing my puzzled expression, she explained that her dad used to be in the Army. A little fellow, he reckoned he often carried packs that were as heavy as him. On an ordinary day, he said, he could march fifteen miles fully laden – but he could carry the same load twenty miles if they had a band ahead of them.

Since those days, he had always encouraged his children to march – or be the band!

'And I was the band!' declared Clara proudly. And if her obvious enthusiasm carried over into her playing, I'm sure her co-workers not only appreciated it but got a lot more done because of it.

We're not all up to making the world a better place, like those good souls doing up their church. We can't all be missionaries or preachers, for example. But in encouraging those who do have such ministries we, too, will be doing God's work.

We could do much worse in this life than follow Clara's dad's suggestion: Either march – or be the band!

Therefore encourage one another and build each other up.
1 THESSALONIANS 5:11

31 *His Bread And Butter*

The church ran a free breakfast club three times a week for those who needed it. Its resources were limited, but it could offer coffee or tea, toast and marmalade, a welcoming place to consume them and someone to chat with while you did so.

After a few rounds of toast, one man, who for years had been dealing with multiple problems, was told he couldn't have any more – they had to make sure there was some for everyone. 'OK,' he said with a shrug. 'I'll be back on Wednesday.' It was Monday.

Sitting with a friend while the volunteers closed up the cafe, he confessed that he probably wouldn't eat again until it reopened.

One of the volunteers must have overheard him. 'Here you go,' he said to the man as he dropped half a loaf onto the seat beside him.

'Cheers! Thanks!' the man said. 'Really!' He picked up the bread and looked at it, and then his shoulders slumped again. His friend, whose own situation wasn't much better, asked what was up.

'I have bread,' the man said, 'but no electricity to toast it and no butter to spread on it. I'm grateful – but I'll be eating dry bread.'

'I'll give you butter,' his friend said.

Now, there's no doubt that the church was doing God's work, and bigger operations help many more people in similar ways; but I imagine it's the little acts of kindness – like that half a loaf and that tub of butter – that make Him smile the most!

The bread of God is the bread that comes down from heaven and gives life to the world.
JOHN 6:33

32 *If You're There*

'God – if You're there – make my dad well! Then I'll believe in You!'

A pretty feeble bargain, but it was the beginning of my journey in faith.

And did my dad make a miraculous recovery? No. He fought hard and then he died. So, how did I become a man of faith?

Well, what came next was an enormous feeling of

'rightness'. I thought at the time it might have been shock, but it still hasn't worn off a decade later.

Dad was the mainstay of our family. A strong man, a kind man, but one with no hint of sentimentality. When he left us, our family almost broke under the grief. But, for possibly the first time, we turned to each other. Without his support, we had to hold each other up or we would all have fallen.

I remember my mother telling me for the first time that she loved me. Having forced myself, near the end of his life, to hold my dad's hand, I found it less strange to give her a hug. And so on, all round the family.

Signs of affection that others take for granted became new lifelines for us. And we're better for it now. We're stronger for our weakness.

As for the sense of rightness, I knew for sure that there is no loss in God. It was time for Dad to go, whether it fitted in with our plans or not. It was time. It was right. Nothing could have changed that.

And that gift of peace left me in no doubt – there *was* Someone in charge!

The Lord turn his face towards you and give you peace.
Numbers 6:26

33 *Small Like Me*

Our family is enjoying the arrival of a whole new generation. My mother has new grandchildren and great-grandchildren, and others are on the way. They have given her a whole new lease of life.

Family gatherings are more fun than they have been for a while.

It won't be very long before one of those little darlings is asking the dreaded question: 'Granny/Great Granny, can you tell me about when Dad was small like me?'

I remember when it was my turn for this humiliation: when my impish daughters climbed onto their granny's lap and made that request about me. They knew they could ask it, because Granny outranked Daddy.

And she had plenty of stories. Like when I went skinny-dipping in a flooded quarry and someone stole my clothes, leaving me to run the three miles home naked. Like when our Canadian cousins came to visit and I took them adventuring – only to get us all brought home in a police van. Like when she found me up to my knees in a stream checking if my new shoes really were waterproof.

Oh, how they laughed! Oh, how I blushed!

Now the younger generation can expect *their* children to ask for stories of when Mummy and Daddy were 'small like me'. I wish them luck!

For myself, I can't wait for that ultimate family gathering when I get to sit by Jesus' feet and ask Him for tales of when *He* was small like me. Now, those will be joyful stories well worth hearing!

Jesus did many other things as well. If every one of them were written down, I suppose that even the whole world would not have room for the books that would be written.
JOHN 21:25

34 *The Dog Samaritan*

What can you say that is good about those days when the rain just tips down? Well, for example, there's this ...

Sitting in a coffee shop, waiting for a break in the downpour, I saw a man run to a bus stop, just in time to watch the bus pull away. He put his golf umbrella back up and paced around restlessly for a bit. Then he saw what seemed like a stray dog. It was curled up by the wall and it was utterly drenched.

The man walked over carefully. Perhaps he expected the dog to get spooked and run away, but it didn't.

He hunkered down by the wall, about four feet away from the dog, and held his brolly so it covered him and the patch of pavement between them. Nervously, with a little encouragement, the dog came in out of the rain.

The man dug something out of his pocket and fed it to the dog. The tail that had previously been curled under it started wagging.

The next bus came along – and the man let it go.

Shortly afterwards, the rain eased up and, after a last

ruffle of its fur, the dog wandered off. The 'dog Samaritan' caught the next bus.

I'm sure God gives us rainy days for sound environmental reasons, but I'm equally sure that these days – and other hard times – are also God-given opportunities for us to step up and love our fellow creatures. Even the four-legged kind!

Truly I tell you, whatever you did not do for one of the least of these, you did not do for me.
MATTHEW 25:45

35 *Wrapped Up In Rapture*

Recently, after a big-money publicity campaign, hundreds, if not thousands, of Americans woke up expecting the Rapture that very day. One entrepreneur raked in quite a bit of money by offering pet-sitting services for those expecting to be bodily uplifted to heaven. No pets are allowed in heaven, apparently.

Well, the deadline came and (as you know, because you're reading this) went. Those expecting to see the Lord descend with eyes of fire and a sword for a tongue – well, I just hope someone gave them a hug!

The next day, a friend posted a message on Facebook. She said (and I'm paraphrasing), 'Did you see Jesus yesterday? Were you disappointed? Well, I saw Him. I saw Him looking for lunch in a dumpster. I saw Him in the eyes of a little girl who didn't know which way to turn for safety.

I saw Him in the man holding the hand of a wife who didn't remember him – and I also saw Him in that wife.'

What does it say about us that so many want to see Christ in His glory but don't want to see Him in the dirt?

Despite all the many prophets and predictions, no one knows when the Rapture, the end of this scheme of things, will come. The Bible is quite emphatic about that. But let's speculate. Why would God choose one time to bring the curtain down and not another? Would it be entirely random, or just whenever His patience ran out? That doesn't say much for His grand plan!

I'm guessing that there will be a point to it, like there is for everything else in the universe He's made. Either evil will have conquered this world and the Rapture will constitute a rescue mission, taking the few remaining faithful ones to safety, or love's work will be finished and the Second Coming will be a tying-up of all the loose ends. The Book of Revelation talks about what will happen, but it doesn't say when – or why. But it will probably be a time of completion, one way or another.

Perhaps the prophets of the 'end times' should cast an eye around this world. Does it look as if we are beaten and there's nothing more we can do? Or like we have finished our task and everyone is well fed and feels cared for?

I don't think either of those scenarios is even nearly true.

The work goes on. So, let's get our heads out of the clouds (from which the Lord was supposed to appear in the latest predicted Rapture) and turn our gaze towards 'the poorest of these'. In helping them, we are helping Him. And in not looking away from them we stand less chance of missing Him.

As long as it is day, we must do the works of him who sent me. Night is coming, when no one can work.
JOHN 9:4

. . . .

36 *At The Back Of The North Wind*

Some people think I'm not all there. Some – I hope – think of me with a mixture of love and tolerance. Well, last night I had that explained to me by a man who's been dead for 105 years!

Diamond, a character in George MacDonald's novel *At the Back of the North Wind*, is a little lad who has been playing with the North Wind. Sometimes smaller than a fairy, sometimes larger than the sky, callously loving or passionately indifferent, wantonly destructive but always life-affirming, she carries Diamond from the hay loft that is his bed and, through a series of wonderful adventures, prompts him to question everything he thought he knew.

Then, while the 'real' world thinks he might be dying of a fever, she takes Diamond 'to the back of the north wind', a place where he stays a long time and which he can never quite explain, but which leaves a mark on him. Thereafter, he is a boy apart, one who unfailingly sees the good – or if he doesn't see it, he *makes* it.

He befriends a girl who sweeps crossings on the London

streets so that ladies needn't get their fine dresses dirty and gents can keep the shine on their shoes. When a curious man speaks to them, he is surprised by some of Diamond's responses. Nanny, the street sweeper, taps her forehead and explains that he isn't all there, perhaps as a result of his illness. 'Some folk call him God's Baby,' she adds.

Standing right next to her, Diamond knows he is being talked about as if he were different, but he doesn't mind. And besides, he thinks, 'God's baby' is a very good thing to be!

So, maybe that's why some folk look a little askance at me from time to time. I know it happens and do you know what? It makes me smile. I've never been to the back of the north wind, but I think, in taking him there, George MacDonald meant to give Diamond a little taste of heaven. Well, I can see that from here – and sometimes I get a little closer. It makes me want to cry just thinking about it.

Cry? Like a baby!

Faith isn't a thing of this world. If you manage it so you can have your faith and still seem the same as everybody else, in my opinion you aren't doing it right – you're short-changing yourself. Step up, my friend, and step out!

When worldly people start to think you foolish, then you're heading in the right direction. Did you know the word 'foolish' originally described someone so wrapped up in the love of God they could hardly contain themselves?

So, let your friends and neighbours look questioningly at you. Let them tap their heads and smile. Maybe they will wonder enough to follow you, maybe not.

Then smile and love them wholeheartedly in return. Being foolish, as the world sees it, is often being close to God, and being God's Baby would be a very good thing indeed!

God chose the foolish things of the world to shame the wise; God chose the weak things of the world to shame the strong.

1 CORINTHIANS 1:27

37 *How Do I Look?*

My sweetheart had been shopping and she couldn't wait to tell me about the dress she had seen. It had been beautiful – and such a bargain!

'Well, let me see it,' I said (because I know what's good for me).

'Oh, I didn't buy it,' she replied.

'Why not?'

In a tone of voice I always think should be reserved for wayward five-year-olds, she explained: 'Because you weren't there to tell me how beautiful it looked on me.'

It's a woman thing, you might say. But men are equally in need of admiration. The compliments that matter most will be different for the different sexes, but ...

Why do we, all of us, have this deep, deep desire to be loved and appreciated? Oh sure, some will hide it under a careless, calloused exterior – but they're only hiding it, not doing away with it. Why would human beings have this basic need if there wasn't someone, somewhere, to fulfil it for us? Someone who thinks we are beautiful regardless of what we've done wrong in the past, regardless of the face we wear for the world, regardless of how much we protest. We have the need because He is its fulfilment!

In the end, another trip to the shops was called for. My sweetheart got two dresses and I thought she was more beautiful in each one than in the other!

Now, if *I* could see that, how beautiful must she have looked to the One who created her?

All beautiful you are, my darling; there is no flaw in you.
SONG OF SONGS 4:7

38 *Purply-Pink Pigeons*

It's not like it was a robot pigeon – or a computer-generated bird on a screen! There was nothing interesting about it at all: a grey body, a slightly darker grey head, two black stripes across the bottom of its wings. It pecked around the bus stop looking for crumbs. If anyone else noticed it, they were probably trying not to step on it.

I just happened to glance at it – and its feathers changed colour! The grey around its neck turned to a shimmering electric green!

I'd seen pigeons with green bands on their necks before (or was that ducks?). But now the feathers were grey again. Now shimmering green.

I walked around the bird and, in a slightly different

light, the same feathers became a sparkling purply-pink. Then grey. Then electric green. Then sparkling purply-pink.

The whole thing reminded me of those T-shirts you used to get that changed colour with your body heat. Weren't they amazing? (No? All right ...)

We think humankind can do a lot of cool stuff – and we can! – but all the coolest stuff has already been done, in the smallest corner of the natural world or the furthest reaches of the universe. Like, for instance, feathers that change colour.

Cool as we are, we're really only just at the beginning – driven by an urge many of us don't understand.

We're not really doing anything new; we're just trying to catch up. Who with? The One in whose ever-changing-but-always-the-same image we were made.

He performs wonders that cannot be fathomed, miracles that cannot be counted.
JOB 5:9

39 *Better Roses*

When I saw the young evangelist setting up his whiteboard outside the shopping centre, I had to stop. He had come to my house one day 'to convert me'. We disagreed on lots of points, but his love of God was never in question.

Written on his board were the words 'If God exists, why do people suffer?'

I could see by the way passers-by were pausing to take a look that this would be a profitable approach for him. So, I asked him how he planned to tackle the subject. He took me to various scriptures, spoke about how some great thinkers had addressed the issue and ended by saying, 'Of course, it will depend what kind of response I get and what kind of questions they come up with.'

I sincerely wished him luck and was about to walk on when he asked: 'How would *you* explain it?'

I'd been doing some gardening that morning and the answer seemed to come unbidden.

'Do you think, if they could feel, that roses would enjoy being pruned back?' He raised a quizzical eyebrow and I continued: 'Do you think they would relish having all that manure dumped on them?'

'I can't imagine they would,' he replied, no doubt wondering where my mind had wandered off to.

'But what is the end result of all that floral suffering?' I asked him.

He stared at me for a few seconds. Then he smiled as the light dawned and we said it together: 'Better roses!'

Consider it pure joy, my brothers and sisters, whenever you face trials of many kinds, because you know that the testing of your faith produces perseverance.

JAMES 1:2–3

40 *Just Say Thank You*

Near Brasov, in Romania, a young Roma woman reached the end of her tether. With no man around to help and no state support, there was just no way she could feed her six kids.

They were already malnourished and she feared they would soon start dying. So, she tried to abandon them. Not just anywhere, though – she tried to leave them with a Christian charity that cared for babies and orphans.

The American woman who ran this charity was confident she could find a way to keep the whole family together, if only the mother could hold on for a few more days. She gave them emergency supplies, then called a meeting of her staff.

Options were discussed, phone calls made and emails sent. Eventually, it began to look as if the director might be able to keep her promise – a well-to-do couple agreed to be long-term sponsors of the family. However, for whatever reason, this arrangement wouldn't kick in for another two months.

And the children didn't have two months.

The director closed the door of her office, knelt on the bare floorboards and prayed.

Meanwhile, I was a happy chappie!

Sitting at home in Scotland, I had just received a sizeable cheque for some work I had done. I was happy because it meant I could pay several bills that had been worrying me.

'Say thank you.'

I looked around, but I already knew the voice was in my head. I recognised it.

'Say thank you.'

So, I spent a minute or two wondering how I should show my gratitude for this provision. Then I recalled some of the stories my daughter had told from her time as a volunteer with a Romanian charity caring for orphans. It worked with the Roma, or 'Gypsy', communities, people so poor their children often took it in turns to go into hospital to be fed. Often, their homes would not have passed muster as garden sheds in this country.

I got on the computer and, through the wonders of electronic transfer, I sent the charity a portion of my blessing, as a token of my thanks to God.

Their thanks arrived by email the next day. The director told me how timely the gift had been, and when we factored in the time difference we realised just how wonderfully God works.

When I'd been hearing that voice, she'd been on her knees asking Him to help a young Romanian mother.

'Well, I hope the money I sent can help her until the sponsorship kicks in,' I said.

'God's better than that, David,' she replied. 'We had already worked out how much we needed to keep that family fed and cared for until their sponsors took over.'

'How much?' I asked, and she told me the figure.

I called up a currency converter on my laptop and changed euros into sterling. But I needn't have bothered. God really is 'better than that'.

My thank you matched her prayer. To the pound.

If you believe, you will receive whatever you ask for in prayer.

Matthew 21:22

41 *Have You Ever Met An Angel?*

Have you ever met an angel? You might think not, but would they really want you to think you had? If we really thought we were in the presence of a heavenly messenger, I imagine that most of us would fall on the floor in shock – and what good would that do?

Les is retired now, but during the war in Bosnia he organised aid convoys that sent hundreds of truckloads of supplies to help the civilians caught up in the conflict. Telling me about the huge efforts involved, he recalled time after time when things had fallen into place as if by magic (or at least great good fortune).

But there was another side as well. Several times his convoys were shot up, and examples of 'man's inhumanity' were everywhere to be seen.

I remarked that he'd definitely been doing God's work and his chin jutted forward. 'I find it hard to believe in God after some of the things I witnessed out there.'

That hadn't always been the case. Les had once been a priest!

I reminded him of what he had told me, maybe half an hour earlier, about how the venture had begun.

He and a colleague had been preparing for a service when they were approached by a young woman in tears. She introduced herself as a child of both sides of the war and made Les swear to God that he would help. He had no idea why she had singled him out. He turned away to make her a cup of tea and when he turned back she had gone. And no one saw her leave.

'And what was it your colleague said about her?'
I prompted him.

'He couldn't get over how beautiful she was!'

'And that was unusual because ...?'

'He would never have said something like that.'

We stood in silence for a moment, then I opened my mouth and said what felt very much like dangerous, worldview-changing words. 'Do you think she was an angel?'

He looked at me sharply, then looked away. His eyes grew a little wider as he stared into the distance.

Les's case was an extreme one, for extreme times. When he said he found it hard to believe in God, I thought: 'Maybe you couldn't see Him because He was behind you, pushing you forwards.'

Perhaps that visitor to his church appeared as a young woman in tears because that was the best way to appeal to a father. Who knows?

But God's work was done in the Balkans despite the worst efforts of man.

Perhaps Les's faith was a price God was prepared to pay to get that work done. Or perhaps, years later, He sent a stranger along to jog Les's memory with the question 'Do you think she was an angel?'

In the visions I saw while lying in bed, I looked, and there before me was a holy one, a messenger, coming down from heaven.

DANIEL 4:13

42 *A Bunch Of Amateurs*

Jane, the choir mistress, doesn't beat about the bush. She says what she means – which is just as well really because the choir are a mixed bunch; glad to be there but with a wide range of abilities and experience!

Despairing of getting her point across to them, Jane put her music book down and swept her hair from her face. She paced up and down in front of the ranks of singers for a moment, then said: 'Does anyone know what the word "amateur" means?'

Sitting over to one side as I was, I saw several confused faces give way to expressions of disappointment and hurt. Surely she wasn't going to insult the whole choir?

Then Jane explained.

'The word "amateur" comes from *amator*, the Latin for "lover", and it means someone who does a thing for the love of it. That's how I want you to sing. Like you love doing it! If you look as if you love what you're doing, your audience are more likely to love it as well.'

Those faces brightened considerably as everyone realised that they did, in fact, love what they were doing and they could, in fact, show it!

Leaving the church, it struck me how well those words applied to evangelism. Given that our faith is in Love, there's no reason at all why we shouldn't look as if we love sharing it. And, hopefully, our audience, whoever they are, will love it as well.

Let's hear it for the amateur!

Many waters cannot quench love; rivers cannot sweep it away. If one were to give all the wealth of one's house for love, it would be utterly scorned.
Song of Songs 8:7

43 *The Road To The Road*

We were driving along when young Chloe asked about the old wall that ran parallel to the pavement. Some time ago, a long stretch of it had been lowered to about three feet high to make it easier to maintain. Now parts of it were overgrown with shrubbery. It was so neglected, I was surprised that she'd even noticed it.

With wisdom born of age, I explained that the road we were travelling on would never have been there without the wall. It had once formed the boundary of a grand estate and the commoner folk would skirt round it as they travelled to and fro between the towns on either side.

Long before cars, there would have been horse-drawn carts going from town to town, I explained. Before tarmac, there would have been a track. Before the track and the carts, there would have been people walking on a dirt path. And before the dirt path there would have been grass growing there.

'So,' Chloe thought out loud, 'there must have been one person who was the first to walk along this way.

And then others followed.' I agreed and she laughed.
'So, it's a good job for us he knew where he was going!'
   Perhaps we should all try and walk a righteous path,
I thought to myself. After all, like that first pioneer who
gave Chloe and me our road to travel on, we never know
who will follow in our tracks!

*I am the LORD your God, who teaches you what is best
for you, who directs you in the way you should go.*
ISAIAH 48:17

44 *A Little Light*

You know those little white stones that often dot
black tarmac pavements? You will probably have
seen them so often you hardly notice them any
more – and yet they perform a vital function.
   When civil engineers were first experimenting with
tarmac surfaces, they laid mile after mile of molten tar,
flattened it and let it harden. As an alternative to walking
in the dirt, or driving along muddy, rutted roads, it must
have seemed pretty amazing.
   But black tarmac soaks up a lot of heat on a sunny day
and then cools down again during the night. Eventually,
the expansion and contraction will make it crack. Then
the cracks spread, getting longer and wider; dirt gets in,
and weeds grow and cause more damage still.
   But if a crack hits one of those little white stones –

it stops! So, the more white stones there are, the longer the tarmac stays sound.

Isn't it amazing how, in so many ways, a little light in the darkness stops everything from falling apart?

You were once darkness, but now you are light in the Lord. Live as children of light.
EPHESIANS 5:8

45 *A Malory Miracle*

'So ... Should I take them or not?'

Fourteen-year-old Jenna was clearing out her old books and taking them to the charity shop. She had already filled two bags, but one box set was proving problematic. It was her collection of Enid Blyton's 'Malory Towers'. The books had been firm favourites when she was younger and she had hoped that someone else would get the chance to enjoy them – but one had gone missing.

Despite several extensive searches, she could only find books two to six. *First Term at Malory Towers* had disappeared. So, the question was: should she take along an incomplete set or put the whole lot in the recycling bin? Would it be appreciated if she took them, or would the people in the shop just think her foolish?

Convinced that doing something was better than doing nothing (but still a little embarrassed), she took the books to the charity shop and explained the situation to the woman behind the counter.

The woman said it would be fine. Then she had a thought and walked to the children's bookshelves. She examined them for a moment and then laughed. Pulling out a paperback, she said: 'It's the only Enid Blyton we have.'

It was *First Term at Malory Towers*!

'We shouldn't be afraid that what we have to offer isn't good enough,' Jenna told me afterwards, all wise with worldly experience as she now was. 'Sometimes God just wants us to try – before He steps in and makes what we have to offer even better!'

Taking the five loaves and the two fish and looking up to heaven, he gave thanks and broke them. Then he gave them to the disciples to distribute to the people.
LUKE 9:16

46 *Looking Redeemed*

Heading for court, I was wearing jeans and an old sweater. My sweetheart, bless her, suggested that with a shaved head and three days' worth of stubble I looked more like a criminal than a potential juror.

She dug out the instructions I'd been sent. They said that 'dress should reflect the importance of what we were trying to achieve'.

A white shirt, polished shoes and a shave later, she allowed me to leave the house.

Walking away, I remembered those words that are often attributed to the philosopher Friedrich Nietzsche: 'If you want me to believe in your Redeemer, you're going to have to look a lot more redeemed.'

It's true. Many believers seem to think their faith such a sober thing that laughter might undermine it. But to know the love of God is a fantastic, joyful thing – we shouldn't be shy to delight in it!

Sharing the gospel is the most important job in the world and we do it no service by making it seem a chore. Let's remember that the good news is actually great news, well worth celebrating – and if we celebrate our faith joyfully, others will join in.

After my makeover, my respect for our justice system was plain for all to see. I can only hope that my love for God and my sheer appreciation of all He has done for me are even more apparent.

Let's take Nietzsche's advice. For the sake of all those others out there, let's look redeemed!

May the God of hope fill you with all joy and peace as you trust in him, so that you may overflow with hope by the power of the Holy Spirit.
ROMANS 15:13

47 *I Pray He Comes Home*

My brother was missing.

Graham had gone south in search of work. His letters and phone calls grew fewer, and then stopped. For the next year and a half, my mum and dad worried and wondered. We had to do something!

Money was tight, but the family scraped enough together for me to travel to his last known address. I planned to spend the night walking the streets.

I had never been to this city before and I wandered around trying to get the lie of the land. I asked a couple of policemen and some security guards where I would be most likely to find down-and-outs and drug addicts after dark. I put cards in phone boxes and shop windows asking Graham to get in touch.

I found a Salvation Army hostel – I knew they did good work with the homeless and runaways. I explained my mission to the officer in charge and showed her a photo. She took it to another room to show her colleagues, leaving me sitting in a TV lounge with a bunch of rough-looking guys.

One of them asked me roughly what I was doing there and in a shaky voice I told them. The mood changed completely. They wished me all the best and gave me some advice. One of them even hugged me!

By now I was getting really emotional. It was getting dark outside, and I was bracing myself for a night on the streets.

The Salvation Army woman returned, shaking her head. None of her colleagues recognised him. 'But that could be a good thing,' she tried to reassure me.

I thanked her and made to leave, but she took my arm and said: 'Let's pray for him.'

I wasn't a Christian at the time and I didn't want to waste time praying, but she was a nice woman and I had no wish to be rude.

She prayed, and I worried some more.

As soon as she was finished, I made for the door. I was reaching for the handle when it opened and a young man came in. He was one of their volunteers, about the same age as my brother. The Salvation Army woman said, 'One last try before you go!' and she showed this young man the photo.

'That's Grrraham!' he said, putting on a Scottish accent. I explained that I was his brother – from Scotland.

'Well, wait here ten minutes and I'll bring him to you,' he said. And he did.

It turned out that Graham was fine. There was no deep, dark secret. He wasn't living rough. He'd just forgotten to write. Or phone. For eighteen months!

Hundreds of miles from home, in a place I'd never been before, a good woman said a prayer I didn't believe would work. And ten minutes later I'd seen it answered.

My brother came home!

We had to celebrate and be glad, because this brother of yours was dead and is alive again; he was lost and is found.

Luke 15:32

48 *Bee On A Bike*

It was a glorious day, so I went out for a cycle round a nearby country park.

I was flying along the path, loving the sun and the music in my earphones and the wind in my (non-existent) hair, when a bee flew into me.

It didn't hit me, though. It was caught in the cushion of air I was pushing ahead of me between my arms and my body, and so it ended up buzzing and twisting and turning two inches from my chest.

I was moving at speed and it was moving right along with me, getting madder and madder!

It couldn't escape and I didn't know what to do, so we both just kept going. Eventually, I recovered my composure enough to let go of one handlebar and hold my arm back. The cushion of air flowed away round my side and was gone, much to my relief and, I'm sure, the bee's!

Of course, I almost fell off my bike in the process.

But don't we often find ourselves ploughing on and on, stuck in a bad situation, heading for a crash? We think we need to be doing something different but, because we're scared of what we don't know, we just keep going, doing the same self-destructive things.

I ought simply to have stopped the bike and trusted I wouldn't get stung.

So, can I make a spiritual point out of all that?
Of course I can.

Bee still!

The Lord will fight for you; you need only to be still.
Exodus 14:14

49 *In The Shadow*

The sun was beating down and the dogs were walking with their tongues hanging out. Harry and I were strolling behind them when he stopped. I turned to see what he was doing and he didn't seem to be doing anything.

Closer inspection, however, revealed a worm on the path. The heat and the dust down there had coated the little thing and dried it out. It seemed to be trying to flip and flop its way towards the grass and whatever life-giving moisture might be found there.

Harry smiled at me, held up a finger and waited. After a puzzling moment, I realised he was using his shadow to protect the worm. Just by standing there still, he kept the dehydrating sun off the little creature and perhaps, just perhaps, gave it the break it needed to make it into the grass.

The worm might have made it anyway. But Harry saw a chance to help and he wasn't about to walk on past while he could be of assistance to even a creature as insignificant as one that spent its life wriggling in the dirt.

I thought of the people in the book of Acts who hoped to be cured by the touch of Peter's shadow and I wondered what it must be like to live life in such a way that even your very shadow may be used for the purposes of good.

As a result, people brought those who were ill into the streets and laid them on beds and mats so that at least Peter's shadow might fall on some of them as he passed by.

ACTS 5:15

50 *Companion In The Storm*

Jimmy was an experienced shepherd, the son and grandson of shepherds, but this was a serious snowstorm. In the days before there were such things as all-terrain vehicles, Jimmy did what shepherds have done for centuries. He pulled his collar up and the brim of his hat down. He whistled for Bracken, his collie, and they started walking.

The flock couldn't be left out there in that weather.

Unfortunately, snow has a way of hiding landmarks, blanketing streams and smoothing out the bumps in the land. It can also close in on you, causing a 'white-out' so you barely know which way is up and which is down.

A lifetime of experience should have told Jimmy not to even try, but he was a shepherd and his flock needed him.

The sheep weren't where he had hoped they would be, and the snow had covered all the tracks. He had no alternative but to start searching randomly.

Soon, any sense of where he was began to fade, followed, gradually, by his strength. He started to wonder if he would ever find his sheep – or see his wife again.

Staggering through the snow, he found a trail and followed it. An hour or so later, he realised he had been walking in his own footsteps.

In despair, he decided to salvage all he could. He turned to the dog, who had accompanied him all the way, and said: 'Go home, Bracken! Go home!'

Bracken set off – but slowly, always staying within Jimmy's sight. Swaying and stumbling, he followed her.

Bracken made it home, but she took Jimmy with her. And on the way she found the sheep!

Jimmy did see his wife again and forty years later she hugged him as he told me this story, still emotional at the memory.

A wonderful true story. But Bracken was only doing what sheepdogs do.

On a grander scale, when the disciples were lost and their strength was failing, Jesus sent them the Holy Spirit. Close as Bracken walked to Jimmy, the Companion is closer to each one of us. All we have to do is stop relying on ourselves, stop walking in our own footsteps and trust our heaven-sent Guide.

It's He who will see us all safely home, no matter how hopelessly confusing the storm of life becomes.

Do not fear, for I am with you; do not be dismayed, for I am your God. I will strengthen you and help you; I will uphold you with my righteous right hand.
ISAIAH 41:10

51 *A Gentle Knight For Peace*

On my journey to faith, various people 'accidentally' walked into my life and made a difference. And no one more so than Patricia Russell.

I was a journalist doing an article on the Eric Liddell Centre in Edinburgh and for some unknown reason she had gone there just to meet me. She had travelled a long way to do so, though she never told me why.

Patricia was the daughter and granddaughter of missionaries and ministers, and had promised herself she was going to have nothing to do with either. She eventually married a minister and went on missions!

Faith was like an irresistible force with her and, just sitting in her company, I felt I was in the presence of something incredibly real. I was a cynical atheist at the time, but she was very hard to be cynical with, or about.

A daughter of God, her other claim to fame was being the eldest daughter of Eric Liddell.

Her father was one of the two main characters in the film *Chariots of Fire*. He was the sprinter who gave up the likely prospect of an Olympic gold medal because it would have meant competing on the Sabbath. He preached in a local church instead – and then went on to set a new world record in a different event.

It's said that when he was actually on the starting blocks for that race, he was handed a note by someone from the American team that quoted 1 Samuel 2:30: 'Those who honor me I will honor.'

A year after the Olympics, Liddell turned his back on his celebrity to embark on missionary work in China.

His daughter told me what she thought would have happened if he had run on that Sunday. 'He would have lost. Something important to him – and in him – would have been broken.'

But it wasn't broken. After his death, Liddell was often referred to as a 'gentle knight for peace'.

Patricia beautifully communicated the same mixture of peace and strength, though it was starting to dawn on me that none of it was really hers, just as none of it had really been her father's. It was all the gift of Jesus.

Looking back, I realise that our encounter was no accident. I went home wanting to know more about this Jesus, who evidently gave such wonderful gifts that nothing the world had to offer could compete with them.

Now I'm running my own race. I've stumbled many times, but less often now as I've come to know better the Source of those good things. Hopefully, I will stay strong – and gentle. And if I can't be a knight for peace, I'll settle for being a squire to my Lord.

And if I meet Eric Liddell when this life is over, I hope he will tell me I ran a good race. That would be a far greater reward than any gold medal.

I will be able to boast on the day of Christ that I did not run or labour in vain.
PHILIPPIANS 2:16

52 *Small World, Big Family*

How often have you heard the expression 'It's a small world!'? My brother lives in a small town in Scotland. On holiday in Cuba once, he found himself on a sun lounger next to someone who lived in the same street as him. What do you think they said? 'It's a small world!'

I sometimes contribute short, inspirational pieces for gift books. They're published in America and I get a few complimentary copies sent to me. Recently, I found myself scrabbling for a birthday present for a friend. I had thought there was plenty of time, but his wife sprang a surprise trip to America on him the week before his birthday and – feeling bad for inconveniencing me (but not very) – she suggested I get him a book to read on the plane.

I wrapped up one of the books my publisher had sent me. (I know ... cheapskate!)

Now, my friend is a Londoner and I'm a Scot. Reading the book on the plane, he recognised the name of another contributor, an American. It was the minister who had baptised him!

My friend emailed me. I emailed the publisher. He emailed the other contributor. The other contributor emailed my friend. And they met up the next day. They hadn't seen each other for 30 years.

My friend said: 'It's a small world!'

I wonder when we will stop being surprised at what a small world it is and just accept instead that we are all one, big family – that we are all God's family!

For this reason I kneel before the Father, from whom every family in heaven and on earth derives its name.
EPHESIANS 3:14–15

53 *Have A Treat*

Frank was fresh off the moors with his collie, Jess, when we met in the street and he invited me in for a cuppa. He put the kettle on and we chatted about the joys of a brisk winter day. Then we made our way to the living room and settled into armchairs.

Jess waited in her basket until Frank called her over. He dug some dog treats out of his trouser pocket and placed one on his knee.

Jess sat in front of him until he gave the command. Then she snapped that treat up and looked, expectantly, for another.

Frank put out a second one. Jess waited. Frank said, 'Take it!' and the treat disappeared. And again.

Jess is a very well-behaved dog, but something else had captured my attention.

I had noticed that, throughout it all, she hardly looked at the treats. She was almost completely focused on her master, waiting to be told it was OK to go ahead.

Sometimes, we humans pay too much attention to the treats of this life. Sure, they bring short-term pleasure, but all too often they come with corresponding fears and insecurities. 'Should I or shouldn't I?' is a question that often nags at us.

For certainty and peace of mind, perhaps we could take a lesson from Jess and look beyond the immediate treat, focusing instead on the One from whom all our rewards ultimately come.

Then we will know for sure that they are earned – and given in love.

Sovereign L<small>ORD</small>, you are God! Your covenant is trustworthy, and you have promised these good things to your servant.
2 S<small>AMUEL</small> 7:28

54 *Stop Along The Way*

Faith is a journey and, especially at the beginning of that journey, it can be easy to think you might never make it all the way.

My daughter Nicola was very new in her walk with God when she went to Romania. The other women she had volunteered with were already making a difference for the Lord. Nicola wondered if she would ever have what it was they had.

The house she shared there was on top of a very steep hill, but the shops were at the bottom. Going for groceries was easy but coming back wasn't much fun, especially as they were also carrying bottled drinking water.

Unless they wanted to take a very long, circuitous route, they had to walk up a 112-step stairway. It was a difficult climb carrying groceries. So, when Nicola ran out of breath, she'd stop and look away from what still lay up ahead of her. Instead, she'd look at how far she had come already and say, 'Well done! And thank God!' The break – and that little feeling of achievement – gave her the strength to climb the rest. Gradually, these breaks came higher and higher up the stairway, until for the first time she made it all the way without stopping.

Don't compare yourself with those ahead of you, or worry about how far you have still to climb. Remember that in taking even the first step towards God you have already climbed a mountain. Pat yourself on the back, take your Guide's hand and you will surely make it all the way!

May the Lord direct your hearts into God's love and Christ's perseverance.
2 THESSALONIANS 3:5

55 *Awake In The Night*

He was just another drunk who had wound up in hospital at the weekend, so why was he crying about letting everyone down?

Eventually – because three in the morning can be a dangerous time when you're that emotional – I pulled back the curtain between us and asked him why he was being so hard on himself.

He told me he'd been drinking with friends and had passed out in the street.

'It must have been quite a session,' I said.

'It's only the second time in my life I've drunk alcohol!'

I asked him why he'd taken it to such an extreme, and he explained that lately 'the pressure had all got too much' for him.

'What does a twenty-year-old know about pressure?'

I asked. He told me he'd been working a lot of twelve-hour shifts. I sympathised – but that didn't justify getting paralytic!

He'd been working all those shifts because his mum needed the money. He was also a full-time college student. He wanted to be a construction projects manager so that he could make a good life for his mum.

'Why are all your answers about your mum?' I asked.

'Because she's disabled and I've been her sole carer since I was seven.'

Wow! No wonder he'd needed to blow off steam!

It seemed that they really needed the money he'd blown on his binge, which was why he was so distraught. So, I talked to him through the early hours, trying to rebuild his self-esteem. I told him he'd messed up badly, but it wasn't surprising. And he certainly wasn't alone in doing that! I told him I was sure his mum loved him and I knew that God loved him.

He fell asleep, much more contented. When his mum arrived later, angry and upset, I waylaid her. I told her how much her son loved her and what a fine young man she had raised. I gave her a sealed envelope with the money he'd spent inside it. Hugs and tears followed between mother and son. And I left unnoticed.

So, nothing much happened. But when I think of him alone in the night, hating himself, I wonder what *might* have happened.

So, what was I doing there myself? Well, I think God pushed me into it.

The night before, at home, I had been rolling around on the floor in pain. My sweetheart decided it was a kidney stone, the doctor agreed and I was taken to hospital.

Then the pain stopped.

I spent a boring day in bed, and then a long night talking about the love of God and mothers to a poor soul who needed to hear about it.

The next day, my tests came back. There was no damage. There was not even anything that could have caused any damage. I got the feeling they thought I'd been wasting their time.

I may have been. But I was still there for a purpose. God pushed me in that direction to plant seeds of love in a confused and desperate mind.

What do I mean, He 'pushed' me? Well, I'm sure I felt a prod from an almighty finger.

Just there. In my kidney.

In the night, Lord, I remember your name, that I may keep your law.
Psalm 119:55

56 *Out In The Rain*

Puppies spend their first few weeks with their mothers, usually in a warm basket; but they do have to leave the house eventually.

When our collie Zara was old enough, we let her out into the back garden to 'water the grass'.

Unfortunately, it was midwinter: dark, windy – and the grass was wet enough!

Zara used to look out of the door – and turn back.
I would put her out and she would sit there in the rain,
looking up at me.

My heart would melt and I'd let her back in. For my
kindness, she would widdle on the floor.

I took to closing the back door so she couldn't use those
puppy eyes on me, but then she would cry, like a baby,
and it would break my heart!

Now she's a big dog. She knows the command and she
knows that the quickest way to get back in is to do what
she's supposed to. It's been years since I've slipped in a
puddle of piddle.

It was worth it.

Which is why, I think, God metaphorically leaves us out
in the rain from time to time. We don't understand what
He's doing, just as Zara had no idea what I was trying
to achieve. All she knew was that she was cold, wet and
scared; but there *was* a point.

God doesn't do these things to us for no reason.
We don't get it, and we cry – but the end result will
indeed be worth it. Even if it does break His heart at
the time.

**In all this you greatly rejoice, though now for a little
while you may have had to suffer grief in all kinds
of trials.**
1 PETER 1:6

57 *Gently Burning*

Come mid-October, our back garden fence faces the rising sun.

'So what?' you might ask.

Well, bear with me ...

We've all heard stories of dramatic, Damascus Road conversions, of people living lives outside society's laws and expectations who found the Lord with spectacular results. But what if you were never that wicked? What if your sins didn't qualify you for an epiphany?

For large parts of the year, my back fence is in the shadow of the house. When it gets wet, sometimes the wind blows it dry but sometimes drops of rain get right into the old wood. Hidden from sight, eventually those little wet patches turn to mould and the wood starts to rot. They're only small, they're not doing much damage, but over time ...

The other morning, I rose with the sun (which in mid-October is pretty late) and as I stood there, making my sweetheart a coffee, I looked out. And my fence was on fire!

Well, that's how it looked. One side was still in shadow, but the other was face-on to the rising sun. The moisture that had condensed on the wood in the night was evaporating, and tendrils of 'smoke' were twisting up into the sky.

In a way, it was being cured. The damp that might have caused it to rot was being burned off. But being burned off gently, without harm to the wood. You could have put your hand on the fence and all you would have felt would have been a mild warmth.

Enough of that warmth and my poor old fence would never rot – but Scottish weather isn't like that!

Which brings me back to those of us who haven't lived chaotic lives; who haven't rebelled against God and society; who sometimes look at the wonderful, life-changing experiences that real 'bad guys' have and feel wistful …

We shouldn't kid ourselves. The little sins we think aren't all that bad are still working away, doing us damage, causing us to rot. Just not dramatically enough for everyone to notice.

Sure, it would be nice to have our shortcomings dealt with in a blinding flash. But there is another, less dramatic way.

Be like my back garden fence!

Just as it spends time facing the sun, so we need to spend time facing the Son.

Find time, as regular as you can manage, and just be there. You don't need to pray, you don't need ritual, you don't need anything, really. Just be in His presence.
Feel the love. Be aware. Be accepting.

Put yourself in its way and the purifying fire will gently burn off the things of this world that would otherwise rot you from the inside out.

Paul's conversion on the road to Damascus was impressive stuff. But he was a tough nut – and he had to hide in a dark room for days afterwards!

Personally, I'd rather be like my back garden fence, on fire in the presence of the Son!

---

*There the angle of the L*ORD* appeared to him in flames of fire from within a bush. Moses saw that though the bush was on fire it did not burn up.*
Exodus 3:2

58 *An Overwhelming Gift*

In a radio interview, a man was asked a fascinating
hypothetical question. If he could have a certain
gift at the flick of a switch, would he take it? (It was
something particular he'd never had before.)

'H'mm ...' he said.

I stopped what I was doing, amazed that he even
hesitated. I hadn't expected that. Surely he should have
jumped at the chance!

Hesitantly, he said yes – but only if he had the option of
flicking the switch off again if it proved too much for him.

And what was this gift, this thing he truly feared
might overwhelm him? It was something most of us
have and few of us really appreciate. It was raindrops on
a window, freckles on the face of a child, dew sparkling
on grass, trees swaying in the wind, a loved one's smile.
The man was blind and the gift in question was the gift
of sight.

It had never occurred to me that sight might prove too
much for someone who had never experienced it!

It made me think about the resistance a lot of people
have to faith.

It's often easier to do without something that might
ask too much of you – and, deny it, deride it or ignore it
as you please; most folk know that faith asks *everything*
of you.

It is indeed a gift that can easily be overwhelming; but
once you've got it, I believe, you wouldn't really want to
switch it off again.

After all, being overwhelmed is kind of what it's all about!

As soon as all the people saw Jesus, they were
overwhelmed with wonder and ran to greet him.
MARK 9:15

59 *AWOL*

Mrs Thomson was a dear old soul whom I met by accident. She'd been shopping and had seen a big box of washing powder for a price she just couldn't pass up. She's in her nineties, though, and she didn't have her wheeled shopping trolley with her, so she only got about a dozen steps from the supermarket before she had to rest.

I walked past, then turned back and offered a hand.

The first thing she said to me sounded like 'It's good to see you're AWOL.'

Surely I had misheard? AWOL, as far as I knew, was an Army term meaning 'absent without leave'. On the long, necessarily slow walk to her house, she explained that she had indeed spent her life in the Army – the Salvation Army!

As a young woman, she had been encouraged to go about her work in company. The same applied to the young men – they would do better to work together, they were told. They could encourage each other and keep each other safe in a dangerous world.

But her superiors recognised that teamwork wasn't always possible, and from time to time they would need to be separated from their colleagues. In which case,

they were *not* considered to be AWOL as the Regular
Army would have it, but were *encouraged* to be AWOL
Salvation Army-style.

'And what does that mean?' I asked.

'Just what you're being,' she said, with a twinkle in her
eye. 'Active in works of love.'

Maybe we should all go AWOL!

**By this everyone will know that you are my disciples,
if you love one another.**
JOHN 13:35

60 *Harry's Flowers*

My friend Harry is an unconscious philosopher.
He doesn't say much but when he does say
something it usually rattles around in my head
for days afterwards.

He's a keen gardener and his flowerbeds in full
bloom are a sight to behold. One sunny day, I saw
him out pottering and wandered over to engage him
in conversation. I got a few grunts out of him in
response to what I'd thought were some fascinating
conversational gambits, but mostly he stood there
shaking his head, as if there was something in his
garden he might never understand.

Well, I wasn't having much luck with any of the
other topics on which I had attempted to engage him,

so eventually I did the decent thing and asked him what was puzzling him.

'What did those flowers do', he responded slowly, 'to deserve to be so beautiful?'

It wasn't the kind of question for which I imagine most folk have a ready answer, but I needn't have worried because Harry supplied his own.

'Nothing, that's what. The beauty was in them from the beginning. All they had to do was let it out.'

He shook his head again and went back to staring. Only, I realised then he wasn't staring. He was well and truly lost in wonder.

I do hope he got indoors before nightfall and wasn't still in his garden in the dark, but his question and that answer certainly kept me awake. He *was* talking about flowers – wasn't he?

I praise you because I am fearfully and wonderfully made; your works are wonderful, I know that full well.
PSALM 139:14

61 *Practise The Presence*

Some churches give out palm crosses at Easter. This particular year, as a new believer, I got my first one. Bringing it home, I decided I would have to find some special, significant place to put it.

Then I forgot about it.

Later, standing in the kitchen, I noticed it had ended up among the dirty dishes. Not very respectful!

Then I thought of Brother Lawrence. A man of humble birth, he joined a French monastery and was put to work in the kitchens. He washed dishes, repaired sandals and did other lowly work for the next fifty-five years.

So, why did more august monks and even bishops seek him out? Why did visitors to the monastery ask to talk with Brother Lawrence as he went about his menial tasks?

Because he practised being in the presence of God.

We talk about God being all-knowing and all-seeing. In theory, we know He must be everywhere. But how many of us can find Him in the little, dirty, boring, unpleasant parts of the day? Brother Lawrence could – and it showed!

He raised everything he did – including washing dishes – to the status of an offering to God. As such, he gave his chores his best and did them with love.

So, I sat my palm cross in a significant place – above the kitchen sink, as a reminder that God is with me always and even those dirty dishes, washed with the Lord in my mind and love in my heart, can be an offering worth making!

Whatever you do, work at it with all your heart, as working for the Lord, not for human masters, since you know that you will receive an inheritance from the Lord as a reward. It is the Lord Christ you are serving.
COLOSSIANS 3:23–24

62 *Jesus Was Busy*

Where is Jesus in this desperate world? Well, mostly He's in all the places we really don't want to be.

Our neighbour was the scourge of the local kids. Any ball that disappeared into his garden stayed disappeared. But all things come to an end, even his localised reign of terror, and age caught up with him.

By the time I was shunted into Mr Campbell's life, he was living on his own with social services providing meals and regular checks.

How did I get involved when he already had such excellent care? Why me, when my wife was a nurse and I wasn't?

Because he was a sexist so-and-so!

When he fell out of his bed and couldn't get back up, he didn't trust a woman to lift him (he told them that!), he wanted a man.

After I'd picked him off the floor a few times, he gave me a key – not that I wanted one. He had an alarm for emergencies, but often the 'alert' people would be ten or twelve miles away with someone else, so they would call me.

Countless times I staggered next door, zombie like, to pick him up and put him to bed. At first I resented it, but towards the end I would stroke the wispy hairs on his head as I tucked him in.

He was still cantankerous and sexist, but I thought he was edging towards being appreciative. Maybe.

Sometimes, before going to bed myself, I would let myself in and stand in the doorway of his living room while he sat six feet away watching TV. His eyesight and hearing were so bad he often didn't even know I was there.

This was a frail old soul. He once broke both his legs brushing his teeth!

Towards the end, his medication made him incontinent and more than once I had to wash him. I really didn't want to be doing that! All my macho pride just screamed against it.

After many hospital visits, there came that last, one-way trip and we never saw Mr Campbell again.

Years later, I told someone about him. Her response started me wondering. 'Do you think he was Jesus?' she said.

Oh, no! He definitely wasn't Jesus.

How do I know?

Because Jesus was busy at the time. He was calming my dread of finding Mr Campbell dead every time I entered his house. He was soothing my pride every time I felt like screaming, 'I'm too busy for this nonsense!' He was helping me be humble when I sat at an old man's feet and listened to his fears. He was repeatedly reminding me that He loved this horrible old man.

No, I don't believe I was caring for Jesus, because Jesus was making the most of what He could find in me to smooth the path homewards for his darling child Mr Campbell.

Like I said: He was busy!

Do not cast me away when I am old; do not forsake me when my strength is gone.
PSALM 71:9

63 *A Help Up The Hill*

I see they're putting a railing up the middle of Tammy Dale's Brae. It's a steep little hill and lots of folk will appreciate the help the railing gives with getting to the top.

Tammy Dale would almost certainly have approved.

Tammy (or Thomas) Dale was a miner who had lived in the first cottage you come to at the top of the hill. In younger days, he was one of the many men who worked in the local coal mines, or the iron foundry the mines fed.

Then an accident cost him the use of his legs.

He could have hidden away, feeling sorry for himself; he could have turned his face to the wall and died. Instead, he pulled himself out into his garden at the beginning of each working shift and waved his mates off with a prayer for their safety. At the end of each shift, he welcomed them back to the top of the hill, congratulating them on another day's good work.

If anyone needed a message passing on, money looking after or children watched for a while, Tammy was the man.

As a miner I'm sure he pulled his weight, but it was only when he started lightening other people's burdens that he really came into his own.

Such was the love for him that, after he died, the hill was renamed in his memory.

Railings are a great help, but there are few things more helpful than a good heart!

Joseph, a Levite from Cyprus, whom the apostles called Barnabas (which means 'son of encouragement') ...
ACTS 4:36

64 *Never Let Go*

I wasn't an inspiring sight on my early-morning dog walk. Unshaven and wearing an old tracksuit, I trudged through mud and wet grass. My dog, Zara, on the other hand, was loving it.

I didn't know it but even then God had a use for me.

The Matt Redman song *You Never Let Go* came on my MP3 player. It stuck in my head, so I played it again. And again. And again.

The previous day, my friend Aurelia had been having one of her worst days ever. Feeling down, she turned on the radio and heard the end of the very same song. It gave her a real lift – but the presenter didn't 'back announce' it, so she didn't know what it was called or who was singing it. She meant to look it up later, but didn't get the chance.

Back on my side of the Atlantic – I'm in Scotland, Aurelia is in New York – when I got home, I went to YouTube, found the video of *You Never Let Go* and loaded it onto my Facebook page.

So, when Aurelia woke up, still feeling low, and checked her computer, it told her I had posted the very song she'd been looking for! It was a much-needed reminder for her that God is always beside her. He'll never let her go.

And it told me something. God isn't just for the big things in life: the emergencies, the disasters. If He has to go transatlantic just to cheer you up – He will!

Are not five sparrows sold for two pennies? Yet not one of them is forgotten by God.
LUKE 12:6

65 *My Father's Arms*

Our minister has a wicked sense of humour.
His sermon was about the men who carried a
bedridden friend onto a roof, dug a hole through it
and lowered him down, all so that Jesus might heal him.

To demonstrate their love, he picked four big men and
had them hold a ten-year-old boy at waist-level while he
did the sermon. While he did a deliberately *long* sermon.

If that boy had been on my shoulders, he could have
sat there all day – I might even have forgotten he was
there after a while. But we were carrying him as if he
was in a litter. Two guys (two lucky guys!) had a leg each,
while I and another fellow supported most of his body
weight. Because we held him in our hands with arms
bent, all the strain was on our biceps.

It was OK for a while, but our minister was set on letting
us feel the full burden of supporting someone in need.

Ow, ow, *ow*! Only pig-headed pride kept that boy off the
ground until the end of the sermon.

Thankfully, he was quite slightly built. When I was ten,
I was bigger and heavier. Back then, my dad was slightly
smaller than I am now. But he still managed to carry me
longer and further ...

Boys like climbing trees, but I didn't much like falling
backwards out of one. I was terrified – until the back
of my head hit a rock. The next thing I knew, I was
surfacing from oblivion in a hospital.

For a while after that, it was all me, me, me. Then the
friends who had shared the adventure with me filled in
the big, black gap for me. Finding his son unconscious,
my dad had picked me up in his arms. He sent the other

kids back home with the news and then set off across two miles of countryside to the nearest farm, where (hopefully) he could phone for an ambulance.

He went cross-country, the quickest way possible: across fields, over fences, through livestock and rough country. And he never put me down once!

In any other situation, I doubt he would have managed it. So, what gave him the strength? Dare I suggest it was love? In what was literally my darkest hour – *all* my lights were out – my father carried me to safety.

Looking back now, from an adult perspective with Dad long gone, I am impressed. It's just one of the ways he impressed me.

I could probably have held that little lad a while longer in church – if I had been his dad. But even if that farm had been five miles away I would still have been carried there safely in my father's arms.

Our fathers and our Father have this in common. Their love won't always be in your face but it's there when you need it, it's stronger than you might expect and it will get you all the way home.

Even to your old age and grey hairs I am he, I am he who will sustain you. I have made you and I will carry you; I will sustain you and I will rescue you.
Isaiah 46:4

66 *Let's Not Be Negative*

Y ou have never seen a kid more excited about adding up and subtracting than Josh.
It was like the world of learning had just opened up for him. He wanted to know more!

He would count toys, tennis balls and place mats, then he would take some away and do a recount to see if the resulting number matched the one he had in his head.

But.

I could tell by his expression he thought he had a question that might stump the greatest philosophers – but he was prepared to give his old dad a try.

'You can't take a bigger number away from a smaller number' – his eyes widened at the thought – 'can you?'

H'mm! The easy answer was 'No', but I knew that in a few more years at school he would learn about negative numbers. Maybe I didn't want him to be taken by surprise. Or, more likely, I just wanted to show off.

So, I quickly outlined how you could take (say) seven away from three, by going negative. The answer would be minus four.

Having impressed my son mightily, I forgot all about it.

Parents' night arrived and my wife and I went to see Josh's teacher. She had good things to say about our boy and she expected great things from him. We tried not to agree too enthusiastically.

As we stood to leave and shook her hand, she dropped the bomb.

'And which of you', she asked, 'do I have to thank for having to explain negative numbers to a class of six-year-olds?'

The teacher recounted how she had explained to the children that you always take the smaller number away from the bigger one. It wouldn't work if, for instance, you took four away from three.

Josh's hand had shot up immediately. He told the whole class the answer would be minus one.

The teacher couldn't tell him he was wrong; but she couldn't tell him he was right, either. The rest of the class weren't ready for that kind of maths. So, she had to advise the children – including Josh – to forget all about negative numbers until they were older.

As she related this, she and my wife slowly shook their heads in synchronised despair.

D'oh! I should have waited. It was too much information way too early in Josh's education. If I had left a little short-term mystery in his arithmetic, it might have avoided a lot of confusion.

The walk of faith is full of short-term mysteries, some of which we will understand with a bit more experience, or after a few more years, and some of which will only be explained in the next life. Just because we don't know a thing yet is no reason to be all negative.

We *will* understand one day. God has all the answers, but unlike some earthly fathers He just prefers to share them with us at the right time!

The unfolding of your words gives light; it gives understanding to the simple.
PSALM 119:130

67 *I Broke Things!*

The church balcony was being remodelled. A wall now enclosed it at the front, behind which there would soon be new meeting rooms and a store room. It was a big job, but the congregation was full of talent. An architect and a carpenter had stepped forward to do the design and building work.

Their skill and industry were being praised at a church meeting when James, who is a big lad with no obvious skills said: 'And I broke a lot of things for them!'

He laughed and so did everyone else. Actually, James had done a power of work. Let loose with a hammer and a crowbar, he had dismantled rows of pews that were built to last, knocked down partitions, prised oak floorboards from their joists and done whatever else the men with the skills had asked of him.

Saying he 'broke things' made James's efforts seem unimportant, but without him clearing the way the work of the architect and the carpenter would have been greatly delayed, and in fact might never have been done.

Sometimes we might feel that our lives are being broken down, or ripped up; but God often needs to demolish a few things before He can put us to new and better uses. Although perhaps, if we 'come easily' and are not fixed too solidly in our ways, He won't have to send James in with his hammer and his crowbar!

You will break them with a rod of iron; you will dash them to pieces like pottery. Therefore, you kings, be wise; be warned, you rulers of the earth.
PSALM 2:9–10

68 *Wonderfully Woven*

We were on a family outing to Stirling Castle. We posed by the cannons, had our photos taken sitting in the thrones and heard the tour guide's tales of murder and intrigue.

Even the tapestries on the walls had stories behind them.

The castle was being renovated and new tapestries were being made on site to cover the bare stone walls and make the castle 'look more lived in'.

In one of the outer halls, the craft workers invited people to join in their weaving classes. Dressed in historic garb and using replica tools, these experts showed their visitors how the draught-excluding hangings were originally made.

At the session we attended, a new version of a design mentioned in some ancient records was displayed, almost complete, picture side up, on a horizontal frame. Then it was turned over.

I was amazed to see how many loose ends and broken threads there were. But the picture side of it had looked fine!

'That's because the strong threads take the strain for the weaker ones,' a craftworker told me, 'and the unbroken threads hold the broken ones together.'

It was an instant metaphor for life.

Leaving the workshop, I looked out across the city below us to the world beyond. Some of the people out there were frayed and broken, but God has provided more than enough 'unbroken threads' to hold it all together.

Leaning on the battlements, I metaphorically tipped

my hat to the Master Craftsman and whispered:
'Beautiful tapestry, Lord!'

---

*My frame was not hidden from you when I was made
in the secret place, when I was woven together in the
depths of the earth.*
PSALM 139:15

69 *I Miss That Feeling!*

Pentecostals. What do I know about them?
Nothing much. I imagine there are parts of their
services I would like and parts I wouldn't. Parts of
their doctrine that would sit well with my soul and parts
I would need to know more about. But, if I was being
honest, I would say the same about my own church.

I do know that Bob, an itinerant preacher of a different
denomination, was wary of them.

Then he and his family moved to a new home in an
inner-city area. Places where his children could play
safely during the day were scarce. Places where they
would get any kind of faith input were even scarcer.

But the local Pentecostal church did run a children's
playgroup ...

With all his defences up, but thinking it was this or
nothing, Bill took his daughter along. He's cautious about
such things, but only because his faith is important to
him. So, he was tense and ready to turn on his heel at

the first sign of anything inappropriate.

He needn't have worried, though – his daughter had a great time. But then, the more cynical among us might think, children are so easy to please. They don't have to worry about doctrinal differences and hidden heresies!

Then again, as it turned out, neither did Bob.

The church made him and his daughter very welcome. Later, Bob would say he had never met such a happy and friendly group of people. Best of all, they positively delighted in talking to him about the Lord – but only if he wanted to! He began actively looking forward to the fellowship surrounding those visits to the playgroup.

After he told me all this, I realised I was still none the wiser about the Pentecostal Church. However, that group in particular, it seemed to me, was doing the Lord's work in a way that would surely make Him smile: working where there was a need, making all comers feel like brothers or sisters and keeping God in the forefront of all their activities.

Bob got a preaching position in another part of the country and he had to uproot his family again. Several months later, he still looked wistful when he told me about it.

'You know,' he said with a sigh, 'when we eventually moved on – well, I don't know who missed that playgroup more, my daughter or me.'

Now, *that* is how to commend your faith in the everyday world! No matter what denominational flag you sail under, present Jesus in such a way that people will miss Him when you, or they, move on.

Leave them wanting more – and let the Lord take it from there!

... we speak as those approved by God to be entrusted with the gospel. We are not trying to please people but God, who tests our hearts.
1 THESSALONIANS 2:4

70 *Luke's Balloon*

How small and unimportant do the details of our lives have to be before God *isn't* involved in them? Frances was heavily pregnant and laden with shopping, and had her three-year-old son by the hand. Despite being told to hold on tight to it, little Luke let go of his balloon – and it did what balloons do on blustery days. It blew out of reach and over a busy road.

Then Luke did what little boys do in situations like that. He wailed.

Frances had to make a split-second decision. Did she throw her dignity and any notion of road safety to the winds and leave her child unattended while she 'waddled' after the balloon? That would certainly make him happy.

Or did she try and get him to see it as a lesson, emphasise the safety aspect of it all – and have to listen to him crying all the way home?

Countless parents have surely faced similar dilemmas. Frances turned it over to God.

As she bundled Luke into the car, she explained the situation the best she could through his wailing.

Strapping herself in, she wondered just how involved in the little details of people's lives God really is. Did He care if Luke's balloon blew away? Did a little boy's tears matter to Him?

She quickly decided that we all have trials to face in this life and God uses them to good purpose. Perhaps Luke would be more careful with his next balloon. She doubted that – but she trusted God.

'Thy will be done, Lord,' she whispered.

She eased the car into the traffic, drove a couple of hundred yards and turned a corner – and pulled over to the pavement.

She opened the car door, stepped out, got back in and gave Luke his balloon.

The wind had dropped and Luke's balloon had been hanging there, above the pavement, so close she only had to reach over the car door and take hold of the string!

No undignified dash through the traffic. No putting her son at risk.

I guess that Luke was too excited about getting his balloon back to thank God but, knowing Frances, I imagine she would have thanked Him in amazement before she even got back in the car.

Anyone with a mind to can dismiss it as a simple coincidence, but she had walked with God long enough to know that there are no such things as coincidences. She'd asked a question – and God had answered it.

Now she knows.

There are no details of our lives so small that God is not involved in them. Just as the sun, which holds massive, far-flung planets secure in their orbits, also causes the flowers to open in the morning, so God, who teaches us through our trials, will also direct and calm the wind just to give a little boy his balloon back.

And we know that in all things God works for the good of those who love him, who have been called according to his purpose.
ROMANS 8:28

National Distributors

UK: (and countries not listed below) CWR, Waverley Abbey House, Waverley Lane, Farnham, Surrey GU9 8EP. Tel: (01252) 784700 Outside UK (44) 1252 784700 Email: mail@cwr.org.uk

AUSTRALIA: KI Entertainment, Unit 21 317-321 Woodpark Road, Smithfield, New South Wales 2164. Tel: 1 800 850 777 Fax: 02 9604 3699 Email: sales@kientertainment.com.au

CANADA: David C Cook Distribution Canada, PO Box 98, 55 Woodslee Avenue, Paris, Ontario N3L 3E5. Tel: 1800 263 2664 Email: sandi.swanson@davidccook.ca

GHANA: Challenge Enterprises of Ghana, PO Box 5723, Accra. Tel: (021) 222437/223249 Fax: (021) 226227 Email: ceg@africaonline.com.gh

HONG KONG: Cross Communications Ltd, 1/F, 562A Nathan Road, Kowloon. Tel: 2780 1188 Fax: 2770 6229 Email: cross@crosshk.com

INDIA: Crystal Communications, 10-3-18/4/1, East Marredpalli, Secunderabad – 500026, Andhra Pradesh. Tel/Fax: (040) 27737145 Email: crystal_edwj@rediffmail.com

KENYA: Keswick Books and Gifts Ltd, PO Box 10242-00400, Nairobi. Tel: (020) 2226047/312639 Email: sales.keswick@africaonline.co.ke

MALAYSIA: Canaanland, No. 25 Jalan PJU 1A/41B, NZX Commercial Centre, Ara Jaya, 47301 Petaling Jaya, Selangor. Tel: (03) 7885 0540/1/2 Fax: (03) 7885 0545 Email: info@canaanland.com.my

Salvation Publishing & Distribution Sdn Bhd, 23 Jalan SS 2/64, 47300 Petaling Jaya, Selangor. Tel: (03) 78766411/78766797 Fax: (03) 78757066/78756360 Email: info@salvationbookcentre.com

NEW ZEALAND: KI Entertainment, Unit 21 317-321 Woodpark Road, Smithfield, New South Wales 2164, Australia. Tel: 0 800 850 777 Fax: +612 9604 3699 Email: sales@kientertainment.com.au

NIGERIA: FBFM, Helen Baugh House, 96 St Finbarr's College Road, Akoka, Lagos. Tel: (01) 7747429/4700218/825775/827264 Email: fbfm_1@yahoo.com

PHILIPPINES: OMF Literature Inc, 776 Boni Avenue, Mandaluyong City. Tel: (02) 531 2183 Fax: (02) 531 1960 Email: gloadlaon@omflit.com

SINGAPORE: Alby Commercial Enterprises Pte Ltd, 95 Kallang Avenue #04-00, AIS Industrial Building, 339420. Tel: (65) 629 27238 Fax: (65) 629 27235 Email: marketing@alby.com.sg

SOUTH AFRICA: Struik Christian Media, 1st Floor, Wembley Square II, Solan Street, Gardens, Cape Town 8001. Tel: +27 (0) 21 460 5400 Fax: +27 (0) 21 461 7662 Email: info@struikchristianmedia.co.za

SRI LANKA: Christombu Publications (Pvt) Ltd, Bartleet House, 65 Braybrooke Place, Colombo 2. Tel: (9411) 2421073/2447665 Email: christombupublications@gmail.com

USA: David C Cook Distribution Canada, PO Box 98, 55 Woodslee Avenue, Paris, Ontario N3L 3E5, Canada. Tel: 1800 263 2664 Email: sandi.swanson@davidccook.ca

CWR is a Registered Charity – Number 294387
CWR is a Limited Company registered in England – Registration Number 1990308

New Every Day
by Rita McLaughlan

These devotional books contain 30 selected Bible passages
and encouraging reflections, along with suggested prayers.
Clear, simple layouts with Bible readings printed in full make
these daily devotionals engaging and easy to use.

God's Unfailing Love – 978-1-85345-650-3
God's Great Faithfulness – 978-1-85345-651-0
God's Compassionate Heart – 978-1-85345-853-8
God's Eternal Gifts – 978-1-85345-854-5

For current prices or to order go to **www.cwr.org.uk/store**,
call 01252 784700 or visit a Christian bookshop

As Time Goes By
and *The Time of Your Life*

by Marie Kane-Dudley

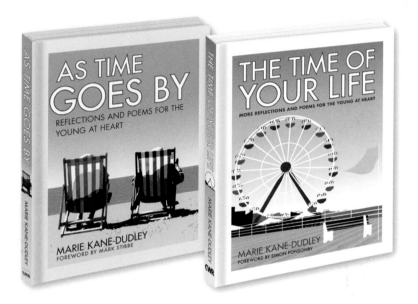

These charming books contain modern day parables, personal stories, poems and reflections that will bring insight, humour and real-life wisdom to readers young and old!

As Time Goes By – 978-1-85345-487-5
The Time of Your Life – 978-1-85345-682-4

For current prices or to order go to **www.cwr.org.uk/store**, call 01252 784700 or visit a Christian bookshop

Courses and seminars

Publishing and new media

Conference facilities

Transforming lives

CWR's vision is to enable people to experience personal transformation through applying God's Word to their lives and relationships.

Our Bible-based training and resources help people around the world to:
• Grow in their walk with God
• Understand and apply Scripture to their lives
• Resource themselves and their church
• Develop pastoral care and counselling skills
• Train for leadership
• Strengthen relationships, marriage and family life and much more.

Our insightful writers provide daily Bible-reading notes and other resources for all ages, and our experienced course designers and presenters have gained an international reputation for excellence and effectiveness.

CWR's Training and Conference Centres in Surrey and East Sussex, England, provide excellent facilities in idyllic settings – ideal for both learning and spiritual refreshment.

CWR Applying God's Word
to everyday life and relationships

CWR, Waverley Abbey House,
Waverley Lane, Farnham,
Surrey GU9 8EP, UK

Telephone: +44 (0)1252 784700
Email: info@cwr.org.uk
Website: www.cwr.org.uk

Registered Charity No 294387
Company Registration No 1990308